WRITING

**A Workbook for the
Television Series**

Written By
Alan K. Garinger

The Kentucky
Network

The KET/GED Series is produced by KET, The Kentucky Network and Mississippi Educational Television.

ISBN 0-910475-30-X   2   3   4   5

KET Foundation, Inc.
600 Cooper Drive, Lexington, KY 40502

KET, The Kentucky Network
600 Cooper Drive, Lexington, KY 40502

WRITING

Contents

How To Use This Book

This workbook has one chapter for each of the video programs in the Writing series. Each chapter of the workbook is divided into six parts. Look for boxes like these:

Preview of the Video	**Goal-Setting Exercise**	**Viewing Prescription**
Vocabulary	**Review**	**Quiz**

First, Prepare for the Program ...

The chapter begins with a **Preview of the Video**, which will tell you what the program and the chapter are about. Then there is a **Goal-Setting Exercise** to help you find out what parts of the program will be most helpful to you. Complete the exercise and check your answers. Then read the **Viewing Prescription** to see which of the writing skills you should concentrate on. Finally, study the **Vocabulary**. These definitions will help you understand the material in the program.

... Then Watch ...

If you have read the preview, completed the exercises, and studied the Viewing Prescription and the vocabulary, you should really be primed for the program.

You'll see this symbol, which means it's time to watch the program:

... Then Review and Practice What You've Learned

After you have viewed the program, study the examples and complete the exercises in the **Subject Matter Review** section. These often present information that wasn't in the video. This information is organized so it can easily be used as a reference guide as you progress through the series. Make it a habit to glance back through the early chapters from time to time.

The **Quiz** at the end of each chapter is designed to reinforce what you've learned. Each quiz contains examples of information from previous chapters.

The major goal of the series is to guide you toward more effective writing. Follow the writing lessons carefully. They are developmental. This means that the later lessons build on the previous ones.

Teacher's Introduction

The Writing series materials are designed to present a developmental series of activities for adult learners. The television component introduces concepts through non-threatening, light-hearted drama. The workbook serves as a guide and a ready reference to constantly reinforce the concepts. Accompanying computer software provides practice, diagnoses problem areas, and further reinforces the learning.

The Design

This workbook is coordinated with the 10 video programs. It introduces each program and, through a self-scoring exercise, prescribes viewing emphasis. In this manner, the series helps develop analytical viewing skills. Viewers will gain more from a video program if they have prior knowlege of its content and have specific things to look for.

Because grammar rules are woven into the dialogue of each program, the workbook outlines these same rules. Students can use the book as a reference guide as they progress through the series.

About the Format

Lessons are designed to encourage student independence. The major goal is to afford guided practice which will help students become better writers. This ambitious goal represents a departure from many adult materials, which emphasize multiple-choice questions and proofreading skills.

While each lesson is independent, and following a particular sequence isn't crucial, skills do build sequentially. For instance, spelling is introduced in the first chapter, but spelling maintenance exercises are a part of each chapter. The same is true of writing practice and the chapter quizzes. More composition practice is called for in each succeeding chapter.

The first six chapters of the workbook focus on specific skills. A wide variety of activities provides many different kinds of exposure and practice.

Chapters Seven, Eight, and Nine are synthesis chapters, in which previously learned skills are combined to practice writing compositions.

Chapter Ten is a review built around questions. This approach helps students become more test-wise. Chapter Ten also includes a discussion of how essay tests are conducted and scored.

Pre-Test

This Pre-Test is designed to help you focus your studies. After you take the test, check your answers against the correct answers given at the end. A Skills Chart follows the answers to help you identify the particular skills you need to practice.

Part A

DIRECTIONS:
In each set of words shown, find the mis-spelled word if there is one. If there is no misspelled word, mark answer ⑤. No set of words has more than one misspelled word.

1. 1) beginning
   2) license
   3) likeable
   4) manufacturer
   5) no error

   1. ① ② ③ ④ ⑤

2. 1) hazzerdous
   2) apologize
   3) manageable
   4) tenant
   5) no error

   2. ① ② ③ ④ ⑤

3. 1) unionize
   2) permitted
   3) valadate
   4) fragile
   5) no error

   3. ① ② ③ ④ ⑤

4. 1) original
   2) analyze
   3) feasible
   4) gorgeous
   5) no error

4. ① ② ③ ④ ⑤

5. 1) nineteen
   2) embarassed
   3) deficit
   4) hesitant
   5) no error

5. ① ② ③ ④ ⑤

Part B

This section will examples are to check your knowledge of punctuation. In each set, there are four numbered lines in which a punctuation error may or may not have been made. Mark the item with the error, if there is one. If there is no error, mark number ⑤. No set has more than one error.

6. 1) Harold Jones the night foreman
   2) is in charge of the warehouse
   3) from 3:30 p.m. until midnight
   4) each day except Sunday.
   5) no error

6. ① ② ③ ④ ⑤

7. 1) MEMO: August 9, 1986
   2) TO: All personnel
   3) Turn off all the lights when leaving the
   4) lounge warehouse shipping room and load-
      ing dock
   5) no error

7. ① ② ③ ④ ⑤

8. 1) Letters are to be sent to the following
      places:
   2) Denver, Colorado; Hartford, Connecticut;
      and Lansing, Michigan.
   3) Also send brochures to
   4) Bonn, Germany; Paris, France; and Lisbon,
      Portugal.
   5) no error

8. ① ② ③ ④ ⑤

9. 1) 816 West Lincoln Avenue
        Pine Bluff, Arkansas 71601
        May 5, 1987
    2) Dr. Alice Metcalf Director
        1121 South Capitol Blvd.
        Chicago, Illinois   60690
    3) Dear Dr. Metcalf:
    4) Sincerely yours,
        Anthony Marshal
    5) no error

9. ① ② ③ ④ ⑤

10. 1) "Yes, I will take it," she said.
    2) "Yes," she said, "I will take it."
    3) She said, "Yes, I will take it."
    4) She said, "Yes, I will take it".
    5) no error

10. ① ② ③ ④ ⑤

Part C

*In these
exercises, mark
the number that
corresponds to
an error of any
kind. If there is
no error, mark
answer ⑤.*

11. Did <u>Anthony</u> and his <u>father-in-law</u> both get <u>jobs</u>
         ❶   ❷   ❸
    at <u>city hall</u>?   <u>no error</u>
          ❹   ❺

11. ① ② ③ ④ ⑤

12. <u>Mary and Bill</u> always spend the <u>Winter</u> in
          ❶   ❷
    <u>southeastern</u> <u>Florida</u>.   <u>no error</u>
          ❸   ❹   ❺

12. ① ② ③ ④ ⑤

13. Many of the <u>customs</u> of the <u>Old West</u> came from
                   ❶   ❷
    <u>necessity</u> and <u>common</u> sense.   <u>no error</u>
        ❸   ❹   ❺

13. ① ② ③ ④ ⑤

14. <u>Arthur</u> was making an exhaustive <u>study</u> of the
        ❶   ❷
    practice of <u>medicine</u> of the <u>Stone Age</u>.<u>no error</u>
                   ❸   ❹   ❺

14. ① ② ③ ④ ⑤

15. He bought a 1956 <u>oldsmobile</u> to add to his   15. ① ② ③ ④ ⑤
                          ❶

    <u>collection</u> of <u>antique</u> <u>cars</u>.   <u>no error</u>
         ❷   ❸   ❹   ❺

16. <u>Wasn't</u> you <u>supposed</u> to <u>bring</u> <u>me</u> the catsup?   16. ① ② ③ ④ ⑤
       ❶   ❷   ❸   ❹

                                             <u>no error</u>
                                                ❺

17. The <u>flock</u> of chickens <u>were</u> in the yard <u>eating</u>   17. ① ② ③ ④ ⑤
          ❶   ❷   ❸

    <u>insects</u>.   <u>no error</u>
       ❹   ❺

18. I <u>don't</u> <u>know</u> <u>who</u> I need to see to <u>get</u> an answer.   18. ① ② ③ ④ ⑤
      ❶   ❷   ❸   ❹

                                             <u>no error</u>
                                                ❺

19. Both of the <u>swimmers</u> are <u>good</u>, but <u>neither</u> <u>are</u>   19. ① ② ③ ④ ⑤
                  ❶   ❷   ❸   ❹

    world class.   <u>no error</u>
                                               ❺

20. Five <u>dollars</u> <u>is</u> too much to pay for so <u>few</u>   20. ① ② ③ ④ ⑤
           ❶   ❷   ❸

    <u>potatoes</u>.   <u>no error</u>
        ❹   ❺

21. The <u>tank</u> of the bus <u>hold</u> fifty <u>gallons</u> of   21. ① ② ③ ④ ⑤
          ❶   ❷   ❸

    <u>gasoline</u>.   <u>no error</u>
        ❹   ❺

22. <u>Some</u> of the players <u>has</u> been <u>suspended</u> <u>from</u> the   22. ① ② ③ ④ ⑤
       ❶   ❷   ❸   ❹

    team.   <u>no error</u>
                                               ❺

23. <u>Neither</u> Ray <u>nor</u> Bill <u>have been</u> able to find a   23. ① ② ③ ④ ⑤
    ❶   **❷**   **❸**

    <u>solution</u> to the problem.   <u>no error</u>
    ❹   **❺**

24. <u>Martha and Sylvia</u> never <u>agrees</u> with the   24. ① ② ③ ④ ⑤
    ❶   **❷**

    <u>committee's</u> decision about the <u>bazaar</u> tickets.
    ❸   **❹**

                                        <u>no error</u>
                                        ❺

25. <u>Him and her</u> <u>went</u> to the <u>theater</u> with <u>us</u> last   25. ① ② ③ ④ ⑤
    ❶   **❷**   **❸**   **❹**

    night.   <u>no error</u>
                                        ❺

26. <u>They</u>, <u>whom</u> were in the play, <u>went</u> <u>to</u> a party.   26. ① ② ③ ④ ⑤
    ❶   **❷**   **❸** **❹**

                                        <u>no error</u>
                                        ❺

27. <u>I</u> <u>drove</u> my car much <u>faster</u> than <u>he</u>.   <u>no error</u>   27. ① ② ③ ④ ⑤
    ❶ **❷**   **❸**   **❹**   **❺**

28. The <u>cat sat</u> on the <u>windowsill</u> and <u>licked</u> <u>it's</u>   28. ① ② ③ ④ ⑤
        ❶   **❷**   **❸**   **❹**

    paws.   <u>no error</u>
                                        ❺

29. In <u>spite</u> of all the <u>trouble</u>, Bryan <u>was able</u> to   29. ① ② ③ ④ ⑤
       ❶   **❷**   **❸**

    do it by <u>hisself</u>.   <u>no error</u>
             ❹   **❺**

30. I <u>don't</u> think Phil <u>looks</u> <u>well</u> since he was   30. ① ② ③ ④ ⑤
      ❶   **❷** **❸**

    <u>released</u> from the hospital.   <u>no error</u>
    ❹   **❺**

31. <u>It's</u> difficult to tell the <u>Browns'</u> twins apart   31. ① ② ③ ④ ⑤
     ❶   ❷

     <u>except</u> Max is the <u>tallest</u>.   <u>no error</u>
       ❸   ❹   ❺

32. You <u>have to</u> drive <u>slow</u> on this stretch of   32. ① ② ③ ④ ⑤
          ❶   ❷

     highway <u>because</u> of the <u>bumps</u>.   <u>no error</u>
              ❸   ❹   ❺

33. "<u>Whose</u> Afraid of the Big <u>Bad</u> Wolf" <u>is</u> my   33. ① ② ③ ④ ⑤
      ❶   ❷   ❸

     <u>nephew's</u> favorite song.   <u>no error</u>
       ❹   ❺

34. I <u>can't</u> hardly see the road <u>because</u> <u>it's</u>   34. ① ② ③ ④ ⑤
     ❶   ❷   ❸

     raining so <u>hard</u>.   <u>no error</u>
          ❹   ❺

35. If anyone <u>asks</u> about this <u>purse,</u> tell him <u>it's</u>   35. ① ② ③ ④ ⑤
           ❶   ❷   ❸

     <u>her's</u>.   <u>no error</u>
      ❹   ❺

Answers for Pre-Test:

1. 3	2. 1	3. 3	4. 5	5. 2
6. 1	7. 4	8. 5	9. 2	10. 4
11. 4	12. 2	13. 5	14. 5	15. 1
16. 1	17. 2	18. 3	19. 4	20. 5
21. 2	22. 2	23. 3	24. 2	25. 1
26. 2	27. 5	28. 4	29. 4	30. 5
31. 4	32. 2	33. 1	34. 1	35. 4

CHECK YOUR
ANSWERS

Skills Chart

In this workbook, once a skill is introduced, it is applied and practiced throughout the remainder of the book. This chart tells the chapter in which each skill is introduced.

Question numbers	Skill	Chapter in which skill is introduced*
1 through 5	Spelling	1
6 through 10	Punctuation	2
11 through 15	Capitalization	2
16 through 24	Verb and Subject	3 and 4
25 through 27	Pronouns	5
28, 29, 33, 35	Wrong word	6 and 7
30, 31, 32	Adjectives and Adverbs	6
34	Double negative	6

* Chapter 10 is a review chapter which deals with all the major skills.

Chapter One
Spelling

In this first program, you'll meet the people who will guide you through the writing skills series. Our friends will be talking about the rules for good spelling. You will need to listen carefully, because the rules are woven into the dialogue. Be alert to the errors Sonya makes. They are common to many people. If you recognize yourself in this video, don't be surprised.

Goal-Setting Exercise for Program 1

These exercise questions are designed to help you get more meaning from the video.

1. Here are some common words, along with some possible plurals. Mark the plural that is *wrong*.

   1.① ② ③ ④ ⑤

   1) miss — misses
   2) church — churches
   3) chief — chiefs
   4) roof — rooves
   5) life — lives

2. Find the misspelled plural in each set below. If there is no misspelled word, mark number ⑤.

   A. 1) Eskimos
       2) radios
       3) tomatos
       4) trios
       5) no error

   2A.① ② ③ ④ ⑤

   B. 1) kittens
       2) puppys
       3) sheep
       4) utensils
       5) no error

   2B.① ② ③ ④ ⑤

   C. 1) glasses
       2) electrons
       3) boarders
       4) performers
       5) no error

   2C.① ② ③ ④ ⑤

3. On the lines provided, write plurals for the following words.

   A. company   _____
   B. boundary   _____
   C. donkey   _____
   D. story   _____

Goal-Setting Exercise for Program 1
(continued)

4. Read the following sentences. Mark the number of the incorrect spelling. If there is no error, mark number ⑤.

A. The quarterback's <u>moves</u> <u>completely</u> fooled
                        ❶   ❷
    the other team, <u>enabling</u> him to <u>carefuly</u>
                      ❸   ❹
    pass the ball.   <u>no error</u>
                                          ❺

4A. ① ② ③ ④ ⑤

B. <u>Courageous</u> effort by the forest ranger
    ❶
    saved the <u>lives</u> of most of the <u>bison</u> and
               ❷   ❸
    a large number of <u>elk</u>.   <u>no error</u>
                        ❹   ❺

4B. ① ② ③ ④ ⑤

5. Underline the "stressed" syllable in the words below.
   A. ac - ci - dent
   B. ac - ci - den - tal
   C. an - tic - i - pate
   D. an - tic - i - pa - tion

6. Find the misspelled word below, if there is one.
   1) agreeable
   2) noticeable
   3) erasable
   4) desirable
   5) no error

6. ① ② ③ ④ ⑤

Answers for Goal-Setting Exercise:

1. 4	2A. 3	2B. 2
2C. 5	3A. companies	3B. boundaries
3C. donkeys	3D. stories	4A. 4
4B. 5	5A. ac	5B. den
5C. tic	5D. pa	6. 5

CHECK YOUR
ANSWERS

Viewing Prescription for Program 1

Put a check mark by each statement that is an accurate assessment of how you did.

❏ If you got them all right ...

BRAVO! Listen to the spelling rules in the program. Even great spellers can pick up a useful tip now and then.

❏ If you missed number 1, 2, or 3 ...

listen carefully to Arthur's discussion of *plurals*.

❏ If you missed number 4 ...

pay close attention to what Arthur says about *suffixes* and certain *plurals*.

❏ If you missed number 5 or 6 ...

Arthur tells how the *arrangement of letters* affects the suffixes.

NOW
WATCH
PROGRAM
1

Subject Matter Review

The plan used in this series to improve spelling is called the SEE - SAY - WRITE method.

See

Seeing is more than just looking. You must SEE the word on a make-believe video screen in your mind.

Put the word "avocado" on the screen in your head. Now look for any arrangements of letters that might cause you trouble with this word.

Maybe you think that the "ca" is a problem. (We do.) On the screen in your head, emphasize this arrangement of letters.

Make it look like this: avoCAdo. If you still have trouble, fancy up the CA by making it a different color from the rest.

Say

This step is critical. The way we say a word can make us spell it wrong.

For instance, most of us pronounce "avocado" like this: "a-VUH-ca-do." So, we have trouble remembering whether that second syllable contains an "o," an "a," or a "u."

Pronounce each syllable carefully as you look at the word.

Try this troublesome word: "probably." SEE the word "probably" on your mental screen. SAY the word "probably." When you say it, make certain you say the second b. Some people say this word as if it were spelled p-r-o-b-l-y.

Now try "February." First, SEE it on your screen. SAY it. Don't forget that there are two r's in this word.

Write

Writing is the third step in the spelling plan. "Project" the image from your mental TV screen onto a piece of paper and "trace" it several times. As you write the word, say it carefully to yourself.

Get in the habit of using this plan all the time.

Rules for Making Plurals

LEARN THE RULES

You probably won't be able to remember all these spelling rules. We'll be practicing them OFTEN, though, from here on. Remember this page so you can refer to it again as you go through the series.

Most plural nouns are made by simply adding s.

chair + s = chairs
door + s = doors
window + s = windows

However, if a word already ends in s, the plural is made by adding es.

kiss + es = kisses
dress + es = dresses

Also, a word that ends with the sound sh, ch, or x must have an es.

church + es = churches
wish + es = wishes
tax + es = taxes

Other exceptions are words with the ending sound of f or fe.

roof + s = roofs   BUT   leaf - f + ves = leaves

Plurals of words ending in o follow a different rule:

If the o is preceded by a vowel, add s.

rodeo + s = rodeos

If the o is preceded by a consonant, add es.

tomato + es = tomatoes

Plurals of words ending in y:

If the y is preceded by a vowel, add s.

donkey + s = donkeys

If the y is preceded by a consonant, change the y to i and add es.

company - y + i + es = companies

Subject Matter Review (continued)

Put the correct forms of these words in the blanks below.

A. company   B. tomato   C. glamor
D. job   E. begin   F. become
G. interest

PRACTICE THE RULES

Bill has worked in three different _____
                                                              (A)

that process _____. They weren't
                     (B)

_____ _____ in the
        (C)   (D)

_____, but they are _____
        (E)   (F)

more _____.
      (G)

Answers:
A. companies   B. tomatoes   C. glamorous
D. jobs   E. beginning   F. becoming
G. interesting

CHECK YOUR ANSWERS

Rules for Adding Suffixes

Look at how English words and parts go together to form new meanings.

PREFIX	+	ROOT	+	SUFFIX	=	NEW WORD
in-		complete		-ly		incompletely

By learning the rules about how these parts go together, you can improve your spelling skills.

LEARN THE RULES

Subject Matter Review (continued)

If the suffix begins with a consonant, the root word usually doesn't change …

polite + ly = politely
stubborn + ness = stubbornness
hope + less = hopeless
state + ment = statement
help + ful = helpful

… EXCEPT for those words that end with y: Change the y to i and add the suffix.

busy + ly = busily
uneasy + ness = uneasiness

If a suffix begins with a vowel, the root often changes.

come + ing = coming
begin + ing = beginning
active + ity = activity

If the first syllable of a word is stressed, the root usually is unchanged when adding "ing" (or "ed").

offer + ing = offering
offer + ed = offered
suffer + ing = suffering
suffer + ed = suffered
pocket + ing = pocketing
pocket + ed = pocketed
comfort + ing = comforting
comfort + ed = comforted
accent + ing = accenting
accent + ed = accented

If the second syllable is stressed, the final letter is doubled.

begin + ing = beginning
refer + ing = referring
refer + ed = referred
occur + ing = occurring
occur + ed = occurred
expel + ing = expelling
expel + ed = expelled

The <u>ous</u> suffix is one to watch. See how this suffix affects the spelling of these roots. It's best just to memorize these.

advantage + ous = advantageous
   (retain the e)
glamor + ous = glamorous
   (no change)
beauty + ous = beauteous
   (root is changed)

The "I Before E" Rule

"**I before E, except after C**" is a rule we remember from childhood. The rule doesn't always work, but it's a place to start.
   Remember the rhyme:

> **Write <u>i</u> before <u>e</u>**
> **Except after <u>c</u>**
> **Or when sounded like <u>a</u>**
> **As in neighbor and weigh.**

<u>i</u> **before** <u>e</u> **words:**

believe, field, piece

<u>e</u> **before** <u>i</u> **words (after** <u>c</u>**):**

receive, ceiling, deceit

<u>e</u> **before** <u>i</u> **words (**<u>a</u> **sound):**

weight, vein

BUT—these words don't fit at all. You'll just have to memorize them.

either, weird, seize, height, neither, leisure, foreign

Test-Taking Tip

The way spelling questions are asked on tests may make them confusing to you. Sometimes you need only find the misspelled word. Sometimes you'll be asked to read a sentence that has underlined parts. The errors, if there are any, may be in spelling, punctuation, or grammar. Another kind of spelling exercise asks you to find the error in a sentence and determine what correction needs to be made. Here are some examples of the kinds of test questions you might find.

Question Type I: Choosing the Error

In each set of words listed below, find the misspelled word if there is one. No set has more than one misspelled word. If there is no misspelled word, mark answer number 5).

A. 1) January
    2) libary
    3) eastern
    4) fortieth
    5) no error

B. 1) purity
    2) margarine
    3) rapidity
    4) syrup
    5) no error

Answers:

A. 2—library is the correct spelling.

B. 5—is the answer, because all the words are spelled correctly.

Question Type II: Finding the Error

In each of the sentences below, find what is wrong, if anything. If there is an error, decide which underlined part must be changed to make the sentence correct.

The joggers, suffering from the heat, finlly
      ❶   ❷
crossed 10th Avenue to the finish line.   no error
         ❸   ❹   ❺

Answer:

This looks like a grammar exercise, but ② (fin**a**lly) is misspelled.

Question Type III: Correcting the Error

Which of the suggested changes would make the following sentence correct?

Harry is a good tennis player, but he isn't consistant.
1) place a comma after <u>good</u>
2) capitalize <u>tennis</u>
3) change the spelling of <u>consistant</u> to <u>consistent</u>
4) change the spelling of <u>isn't</u> to <u>isnt</u>
5) no corrections are necessary

Answer:

The correct response is 3. Test questions of this type require you to make careful comparisons of the answer choices and the original sentence.

Quiz for Program 1

Now complete these exercises.

1. Here are some words from the video that have suffixes and prefixes. On the lines provided, write the root words.

    A. abilities   _____
    B. usually   _____
    C. unfortunately _____
    D. unlikely   _____
    E. countries   _____
    F. bushes   _____
    G. bigger   _____
    H. heartless   _____
    I. meaningless   _____
    J. stubbornness   _____
    K. beginning   _____
    L. irregularly   _____
    M. hopeless   _____
    N. desirable   _____
    O. unstressed   _____

2. In the exercise below are more words from the video. In each set, choose the misspelled word. No more than one word is misspelled in each set. If there is no misspelled word, mark answer number ⑤.

    A. 1) differently   2A. ① ② ③ ④ ⑤
        2) unfortunatly
        3) pieces
        4) dictionary
        5) no error

    B. 1) heroes   2B. ① ② ③ ④ ⑤
        2) rodeos
        3) iglooes
        4) cameos
        5) no error

    C. 1) immediatly   2C. ① ② ③ ④ ⑤
        2) foolishness
        3) consonant
        4) accented
        5) no error

D.1) beginning   2D.① ② ③ ④ ⑤
   2) permitted
   3) illegal
   4) effectively
   5) no error

3. In the following sentences, the underlined words may or may not be misspelled. Find the misspelling. If there is no error, mark number ⑤.

A. When Jennifer was doing the <u>laundry</u>, she   3A.① ② ③ ④ ⑤
                                    ❶

    <u>accidently</u> washed two <u>cameos</u> given to
      ❷   ❸

    her by her <u>grandmother</u>.   <u>no error</u>
               ❹   ❺

B. The children gave <u>thier</u> <u>friends</u> some of   3B.① ② ③ ④ ⑤
                 ❶   ❷

    the <u>souvenirs</u> they brought back from
        ❸

    <u>Mexico</u>.   <u>no error</u>
    ❹   ❺

C. Instead of <u>worrying</u> about her <u>studys</u>,   3C.① ② ③ ④ ⑤
         ❶   ❷

    Martha went to a <u>relaxing</u> movie with her
                 ❸

    <u>neighbor</u>.   <u>no error</u>
    ❹   ❺

4. In the video, there were examples of the <u>u</u> sound. Sometimes the same letters which make a <u>u</u> sound like <u>oo</u> also make the sound <u>you</u>. In the list below, place a <u>u</u> by those words that sound like <u>oo</u> and a <u>y</u> by those that sound like <u>you</u>. (NOTE: The way you pronounce some of these words may depend upon the region in which you grew up.)

____ stew	____ fruit	____ diffuse
____ few	____ Tuesday	____ fuse
____ ewe	____ sluice	____ canoe
____ flew	____ preclude	____ raccoon
____ juice	____ askew	____ excuse

5. Add the suffix "-ment" to the words below. You may want to look back at the rules for adding suffixes.

A. judge + ment = _____
B. state + ment = _____
C. fulfill + ment = _____
D. allot + ment = _____

6. Add the suffix "-ing" to the words below. Change the spelling of the root word if necessary.

A. ferry + ing = _____
B. infer + ing = _____
C. offer + ing = _____
D. practice + ing = _____
E. ready + ing = _____

7. Many words in English are confusing because they sound like other words but have different meanings and uses. Below is a list of such words, and some sentences with words left out. Put the proper words in the blanks.

accept	means to receive.
except	means to leave out or omit.
advice	is a noun. It is a recommendation.
advise	is a verb. It means to inform.
clothes	are what you wear.
cloths	are pieces of material.
conscience	is the little voice in your head.
conscious	means to be aware or awake.
device	is a noun. It is some kind of gadget.
devise	is a verb. It means to invent.
formally	has to do with ceremony or custom.
formerly	means "before."
lose	means to misplace something.
loose	means not tight or not fastened down.
prophecy	is a noun (PRAH-fuh-sea). It is a prediction.
prophesy	is a verb (PRAH-fuh-sigh). It means to make a prediction.

A. My _____ to you is to sell the
    car before you have any more trouble.
B. She was dressed in her finest new

    _____.

C. I _____ your offer of a new
    job.

Quiz for Program 1
(continued)

D. He put a strange _____ on his carburetor, which allowed him to get extremely good gas mileage.

E. All of the cars were black _____ mine.

F. What would you _____ me to do about this problem?

G. Martha, where do you keep the dust _____?

H. It's easy to _____ your way in the deep woods.

I. The white-haired man in the long robe said, "I _____ the world will end tomorrow."

J. We must _____ a plan to get out of this mess.

K. He was _____ an aide to President Carter.

L. The lie the boy told preyed on his _____.

M. I know him, but we've never been _____ introduced.

N. Be careful of that _____ step.

O. The patient was _____ just one hour after the operation.

P. The minister mentioned a _____ from the Bible.

Answers for Quiz:

1A. ability	1B. usual	1C. fortunate
1D. like	1E. country	1F. bush
1G. big	1H. heart	1I. mean
1J. stubborn	1K. begin	1L. regular
1M. hope	1N. desire	1O. stress
2A. 2	2B. 3	2C. 1
2D. 5	3A. 2	3B. 1
3C. 2		

4. U stew	U fruit	Y diffuse
Y few	Y Tuesday	Y fuse
Y ewe	U sluice	U canoe
U flew	U preclude	U raccoon
Y juice	Y askew	Y excuse
5A. judgment	5B. statement	5C. fulfillment
5D. allotment	6A. ferrying	6B. inferring
6C. offering	6D. practicing	6E. readying
7A. advice	7B. clothes	7C. accept
7D. device	7E. except	7F. advise
7G. cloths	7H. lose	7I. prophesy
7J. devise	7K. formerly	7L. conscience
7M. formally	7N. loose	7O. conscious
7P. prophecy		

CHECK YOUR ANSWERS

Now it's time to SEE - SAY - WRITE. In each chapter, we will give you a few words that are misspelled by many people. You should practice these words until you know them as well as you know your name.

SPELLING DEMONS

A.	does	E.	ninety	I.	benefit
B.	doesn't	F.	ninth	J.	committee
C.	grammar	G.	lose	K.	friend
D.	humor	H.	athletic	L.	decision

Special Demon

REMEMBER: "All right" is two words.

Your Own List

Now go back through the work in this chapter. Find words you think you might not ALWAYS be able to spell.

SEE them. SAY them. Then WRITE them on the lines provided below. This is the beginning of a list we will refer to frequently.

_____   _____
_____   _____
_____   _____
_____   _____
_____   _____

When You Write

Few people want to improve spelling skills so they can enter a spelling bee. What people want is to be able to write correctly.

Pick ten words from various places in this chapter and use them all in one paragraph. Write the paragraph on any subject you like.

_____
_____
_____
_____
_____
_____
_____
_____
_____
_____
_____
_____

Chapter
Two
Mechanics

In this program, you'll see Sonya and Freddy learn the importance of good form in capitalizing and punctuating sentences in several kinds of writing.

Arthur gets a little carried away when he compares punctuation to a road map. But he is right because punctuation can keep you from getting lost when you read. It can also keep you from getting lost when you are following directions, as Sonya and Arthur discover.

Be especially alert when our friends are talking about capital letters. The story goes quickly, but all the suggestions are important to good writing.

English has many rules for capitalization and punctuation. We will introduce you to only a few in this program. When other rules are needed as we go along, we'll explain them. For now, follow the exercises in this chapter.

Goal-Setting Exercise for Program 2

These exercise questions are designed to help you get more meaning from the video.

1. Find the error in each sentence. If there is no error, mark answer number ⑤.

    A. My <u>friend</u>, <u>Wallace</u>, is an <u>expert</u> on the   1A. ① ② ③ ④ ⑤
            ❶   ❷   ❸
        <u>civil war</u>.   <u>no error</u>
            ❹   ❺

    B. The new <u>television</u> I <u>bought</u> is a <u>19-inch</u>   1B. ① ② ③ ④ ⑤
                    ❶   ❷   ❸
        <u>hitachi</u>.   <u>no error</u>
            ❹   ❺

2. Correct any **capitalization** errors in the following sentences.

    A. Is this the right road to gnawbone, indiana?

    B. Esther always spends the winter in warm climates of the south.

    C. If you drive south on this highway, you'll be in west virginia before you know it.

    D. After he was graduated from the university, he went to work for the department of agriculture.

3. Correct any **punctuation** errors in the following sentences.

    A. Susan said bring me the red book.

    B. Is this the right button to push.

    C. Susan had already packed the necessary

Goal-Setting Exercise for Program 2
(continued)

clothes extra shoes a raincoat extra

slacks and a hat.

D.   The extraterrestrial his ray gun pointed

directly at us said Take me to your

leader.

Answers for Goal-Setting Exercise:

1A. 4	1B. 4	2A. <u>G</u>nawbone, <u>I</u>ndiana
2B. <u>S</u>outh	2C. <u>W</u>est <u>V</u>irginia	2D. <u>D</u>epartment of <u>A</u>griculture

3A. Susan said, "Bring me the red book."
3B. Is this the right button to push?
3C. Susan had already packed the necessary clothes: extra shoes, a raincoat, extra slacks and a hat.
3D. The extraterrestrial, his ray gun pointed directly at us, said, "Take me to your leader."

CHECK YOUR ANSWERS

Viewing Prescription for Program 2

Put a check mark by each statement that is an accurate assessment of how you did.

☐ If you got them **all right** …

We're impressed! See if you can identify all the rules discussed.

☐ If you missed **1A** or **1B** …

You may need help with capitalization of **proper nouns**.

☐ If you missed **2A** or **2C** …

Remember, **cities and states** are capitalized. Watch for Sonya's problem with this rule.

☐ If you missed number **2B** …

Regions of a country are capitalized. This rule is discussed in the program.

☐ If you missed number **2D** …

Watch for the explanation of capitalization of **government offices**.

☐ If you missed number **3A** …

Watch how Sonya learns about **direct quotations**.

☐ If you missed number **3B** …

Remember, a question requires a **question mark** at the end.

☐ If you missed number **3C** …

Be alert to what is said about separating **items in a series**.

Viewing Prescription for Program 2
(continued)

❑ If you missed number **3D** …

By the end of the program, you should be able to tell how Sonya knows how to punctuate a sentence like this one.

Vocabulary for Program 2

Some common grammar terms are used in the video and the workbook. It might be a good idea to add them to your spelling list at the end of the chapter.

appositive (uh-POS-uh-tiv) means a word, phrase, or clause that explains a word or expression. *Example:* Harold, the man who cleans the swimming pool, said we need a new filter. The underlined phrase explains who Harold is.

article (AR-tih-kuhl) is a special name for a, an, and the.

conjunction (cuhn-JUNK-shun) refers to connecting words like and, but, or and nor.

ellipsis (ee-LIP-sis) a mark (…) indicating an intentional omission of words.

imperative (im-PAIR-uh-tiv) is a kind of sentence which is a mild command. *Example:* Fill out the order blank and leave it on my desk. An imperative sentence ends with a period.

preposition (preh-puh-ZIH-shun) is a word that shows relationships within a sentence. *Examples:* for, to, with, of, etc.

LEARN THE WORDS

NOW WATCH PROGRAM 2

The rules shown here are discussed in the program. Since you may not remember all of them, keep this page in mind so you can come back to review them.

Rules for Capitalization

**LEARN THE
RULES**

Capitalize ...

... the first words in sentences:

The first word in this sentence is "the."

... proper nouns (names of particular persons, places, and things):

INCLUDING ...

trademarked names, names of products, businesses

Chevrolet trucks, Ivory Soap, Green Giant corn

geographic terms, languages and nationalities

North Carolina, San Francisco, Ohio River, the mountains of South Dakota (*not* descriptive phrases before a proper noun), China, Chinese restaurant, French, German

periods of history, wars, holidays and dates

Fourth of July, Tuesday, Civil War, April, Stone Age, Christmas

direction words when they name a region of a country

He enjoyed the beauty of the West.

don't capitalize ...

... common nouns that are *not* the first words in sentences:

The river is exceptionally muddy today.

... a word merely indicating a direction:

"Go west, young man."

... seasons:

spring, winter, autumn, fall, summer

Subject Matter Review
(continued)

Underline each word that should be capitalized.

PRACTICE
THE RULES

1. there are only a few places in south carolina where gullah is spoken.

2. when you think of the east, you think of new york city.

3. on the salisbury plain stands the awe-inspiring stonehenge, a relic of the neolithic period.

4. it was late in world war II before the germans employed guided missiles.

5. spring begins with the vernal equinox and ends with the summer solstice.

6. the chinatown of san francisco is the largest in the u.s.

7. all directions from the north pole are south.

8. the jewish ceremonies of the passover are among the most sacred rites of this religion.

9. michael jackson was burned during the filming of a pepsi-cola commercial.

10. v.j. day, the day the japanese surrendered, marked the end of world war II.

Answers:
1. There ... South Carolina ... Gullah
2. When ... East ... New York City
3. On ... Salisbury Plain ... Stonehenge ... Neolithic
4. It ... World War ... Germans
5. Spring (only because it's the first word in the sentence)
6. The ... Chinatown ... San Francisco ... U.S.
7. All ... North Pole
8. The ... Jewish ... Passover
9. Michael Jackson ... Pepsi-Cola
10. V.J. Day ... Japanese ... World War

CHECK YOUR
ANSWERS

Subject Matter Review (continued)

Capitalize ...

... first words of complete sentences in direct quotations:

"That is the truth," she said.
He said, "That is the truth."
"That," he said, "is the truth."

... proper nouns (names of particular persons, places, and things):

INCLUDING ...

names of people

Benjamin Franklin, George Washington, Booker T. Washington, John, Mary, Sam

the names of astronomical bodies

Mars, Jupiter, Ursa Minor, Earth

don't capitalize ...

... first words of direct quotations that are not complete sentences:

That is "the truth," she said.
He said that is "the truth."

... common nouns derived from proper nouns:

chinaware, french fries, plaster of paris, quixotic

... "sun" or "moon":

Americans first walked on the moon in July of 1969.
Mercury, Venus, Earth, and Mars all orbit the sun.

... "earth" when it refers to "dirt" or "ground" instead of the planet:

Most farmers are pround of being close to the earth.
John is very practical, very down to-earth.

LEARN THE RULES

Underline the words that should be capitalized.

1. phil said, "you owe me seven dollars."

2. susan gave a painting of the planet jupiter
   to the planetarium.

3. I got this buick at smith's garage.

4. where on earth have you been?

5. general douglas macarthur kept his word to
   the filipinos and returned to free them.

6. bruce said, "tell me where by bic pen is."

7. ancient asians learned the art of applying
   many coats of lacquer on furniture to produce
   a fine surface.

8. the big dipper bowl points to the north star.

PRACTICE THE RULES

Subject Matter Review (continued)

9. the announcer said, "the president will discuss the problem
   of famine in ethiopia."

Answers:
1. Phil said, "You owe me seven dollars."
2. Susan … Jupiter
3. Buick … Smith's Garage
4. Where … Earth
5. General Douglas MacArthur … Filipinos
6. Bruce … Tell … Bic
7. Ancient … Asians
8. The Big Dipper … North Star
9. The … The president … Ethiopia

CHECK YOUR ANSWERS

Capitalize …

… proper nouns (names of particular persons, places, and things):

INCLUDING …

"kinship" words used as parts of names

Uncle Bert, Aunt Esther, Father, Mother

titles used as parts of names (preceeding the names)

President Carter, General Westmoreland, Admiral Dewey, Superintendent Johnson

names of institutions and political parties

Ohio University, Department of Natural Resources, Republican, Democrat, Methodist church (the building), Methodist Church (the organization)

… first words in titles of books, magazines, and articles:

The Life and Times of William Shakespeare

… major words in titles of books, magazines, and articles:

Blue Highways, Life on the Mississippi, The People's Almanac

don't capitalize …

… "kinship" words used only to describe relationships:

her mother, Jim's uncle, their aunts, the father of our country

… titles not used as parts of persons' names (standing alone or following names):

The governor took office on May 4.
Jack Smith, superintendent, attended the meeting.
The mayor spoke to the group.

… minor words in titles of books, magazines, and articles:

Life on the Mississippi, The Life and Times of William Shakespeare

NOTE: "Minor words" are articles, short conjunctions, and prepositions that are not the first words of titles.

LEARN THE RULES

PRACTICE
THE RULES

Subject Matter Review (continued)

Underline the words that should be capitalized.

1. herman melville wrote the novel, billy budd.

2. after he completed his work at the university, sam went to work for the department of commerce in jackson.

3. did your uncle david give this book to my father?

4. teddy roosevelt was the power behind the bull moose party.

5. "where is uncle aaron going?" sally asked her mother.

6. levi coffin's contribution to the underground railroad stemmed from his quaker beliefs.

7. the defendant gave judge steel a u.s. history book opened to the constitution.

8. any congressman who can be returned to washington, d.c. six times must be pleasing someone.

Answers:
1. Herman Melville … Billy Budd
2. After … Sam … Department of Commerce … Jackson
3. Did … Uncle David
4. Teddy Roosevelt … Bull Moose
5. Where … Uncle Aaron … Sally
6. Levi Coffin's … Underground Railroad … Quaker
7. The … Judge Steel … U.S. … Constitution
8. Any … Washington, D.C.

CHECK YOUR
ANSWERS

Rules for Punctuation

LEARN THE RULES

Use a comma to separate items in a series:

Doors, windows, trim, and carpet were ordered yesterday.
The teacher, the principal, the superintendent, and the president of the school board met for lunch.
We discovered that the tree was still alive, that it was growing properly, and that it would probably bloom in the spring.

NOTE: Some writers drop the comma between the final two items in a simple series:

Doors, windows, trim and carpet were ordered yesterday.

But dropping the final series comma creates confusing sentences in many cases (imagine the next example sentence without a final comma!), and is generally not good practice.

The children were given crayons and paper, scissors and paste, and paint and clay.

Use a comma to separate a series of adjectives before a noun:

She was a thoughtful, courteous person.

Use a comma to separate a direct address from the content of the message:

Bill, come sit by me.
So you see, Mother, that's how it happened.

Use a comma to separate an appositive or other type of phrase from the rest of the sentence:

Charles, the man on the left, is a friend of mine. (appositive)
Isaac Asimov, the famous writer, presented the main speech. (appositive)
The burglar, who had his face covered, stood at the window. (clause)
The burglar, face covered, stood at the window. (phrase)

NOTE: The phrases in the examples above are called "non-restrictive" because the sentences would mean the same things without the words between the commas. In "restrictive" clauses, phrases, or appositives, commas are not used because the words are necessary to the meaning of the sentence.

The word "accept" is sometimes confused with the word "except."

This sentence should not be written:
The word , "accept," is sometimes confused with the word, "except."

Place commas where they belong in the following sentences.

1. Watson come here. I want you.

2. Biscuits and gravy ham and eggs and pork and beans are foods we think go together.

3. Archimedes one of the first physicists said "Give me a place to stand on and I will move the Earth."

4. In the cool cool cool of the evening.

5. Insects spiders centipedes lobsters and shrimp are all of the phylum arthropoda.

6. Icarus with wings of wax and feathers soared too close to the hot blazing sun.

7. Will you help me a minute Sally?

8. One element silicon makes up most of the weight of Earth.

9. Thanks to Roger Walter and Ruth we have raised our quota.

10. Martha Johnson who lives on Elm Street bought six books a box of magazines and an old journal at the church bazaar.

Answers:
1. Watson, come here. I want you.
2. Biscuits and gravy, ham and eggs, and pork and beans are foods we think go together.
3. Archimedes, one of the first physicists, said, "Give me a place to stand on and I will move the Earth."
4. In the cool, cool, cool of the evening.
5. Insects, spiders, centipedes, lobsters and shrimp are all of the phylum arthropoda.
6. Icarus, with wings of wax and feathers, soared too close to the hot, blazing sun.
7. Will you help me a minute, Sally?
8. One element, silicon, makes up most of the weight of Earth.
9. Thanks to Roger, Walter, and Ruth, we have raised our quota.
10. Martha Johnson, who lives on Elm Street, bought six books, a box of magazines, and an old journal at the church bazaar.

Use a comma to separate the parts of a full date:

October, 1985
November 17, 1984
Saturday, July 15, 1989

LEARN THE RULES

NOTE: When a full date appears in a sentence, some writers place a comma after the year:

I'll meet you here January 1, 1985, at three in the afternoon.

Use a comma to separate the parts of an address (but not between the state and zip code):

Sydney, Australia
Indianapolis, IN 46021

NOTE: When a city and state appear in the middle of a sentence, some writers use a comma after the state name.

We reached Denver, Colorado, without any trouble.

Use a comma to separate the attribution (who said it) from a direct quotation (what was said):

Harold said, "We are not afraid."
"We are not afraid," Harold said.

NOTE: Don't use a comma when the quotation is not direct.
    Harold said that we are not afraid.

Use a comma to set off an interjection at the beginning of a sentence:

Oh, it really doesn't matter.

Use a comma to offset an introductory phrase at the beginning of a sentence:

Crying loudly, Marcia ran into the yard.
If it were up to me, I'd do it differently.
To be certain the door was locked, he tried it once more.

1. Place commas where they belong in the following sentences.

    A. "Tell me if you can" she said "why you

        are so late."

    B. Yes I think I can do it.

PRACTICE THE RULES

Subject Matter Review (continued)

C. Meet me in St. Louis Missouri April 12
    1985.

D. In regard to that question let me say
    that there is no evidence that you are
    right.

E. No that's not the one.

2. Some of the sentences below are correct; some are not. Place a check mark beside any sentence where commas are used properly. Correct the errors in the others.

A. Brown, Smith and Jones Attorneys-at-Law

    1006 Main Street

    Boise Idaho, 87321

B. Well, I'm not really sure.

C. The famous clown Emmett Kelley thrilled
    circus crowds for more than 40 years.

D. Sally asked "Where do you want this?"

E. In the future when a situation like this
    occurs call the authorities immediately.

Answers:
1A. "Tell me if you can," she said, "why you are so late."
1B. Yes, I think I can do it.
1C. Meet me in St. Louis, Missouri, April 12, 1985.
1D. In regard to that question, let me say that there is no evidence that you are right.
1E. No, that's not the one.
2A. Brown, Smith, and Jones, Attorneys-at-Law
    1006 Main Street
    Boise, Idaho 87321
2B. Well, I'm not really sure. (3)
3C. The famous clown, Emmett Kelley, thrilled circus crowds for more than 40 years.
2D. Sally asked, "Where do you want this?"
2E. In the future, when a situation like this occurs, call the authorities immediately.

CHECK YOUR
ANSWERS

Use an exclamation point to express strong feeling:

Stop that car!

NOTE: Unlike a comma or a period, an exclamation point is placed before a final quotation mark only if the quotation itself expresses the feeling:

The crowd was screaming, "Save them! Save them!"
Stop saying, "I'm tired"!

Use a period at the end of a sentence:

It's time to go.
Please go away.

NOTE: Periods and commas are *always* placed before adjacent final quotation marks!

Use a colon before a listed series:

We wanted to know three things: 1) where we were; 2) where we had been; and 3) where we were going.

Use a colon after the salutation of a formal letter:

Dear Mr. Smith:

Use a semicolon to separate items in a series when one or more of the items already contains a comma:

These cities were still in the competition: Indianapolis, Indiana; Boise, Idaho; Concord, New Hampshire; and Charleston, West Virginia.

Use a semicolon in place of a conjunction that joins two clauses:

The weather was beautiful, but the clouds were beginning to fade.
The weather was beautiful; the clouds were beginning to fade.

LEARN THE
RULES

1. Add or cross out the punctuation in these examples. There may not be errors in some of them.

A. Phil go to the stock room and pick up the following 4 boxes of M2-387 2 boxes of D430Y and 2 boxes of LDA73

B. Dear Ms. Andrews:

PRACTICE
THE RULES

Subject Matter Review (continued)

C. "You'll find them listed in the directory as Wilson Thomas A Martin Marcia L Thorndike Robert C and Anthony Susan D

D. Stop thief

E. He looked in the cupboard for some crackers there were none

2. Here is a copy of Sonya's note to Arthur. See if you can correct it now.

dear arthur,

here is the box of fine fin fish food you asked me to pick up at the foodway store on lexington avenue. It costs so much to feed your hungry fish that I think you should say to them swim South for the Winter. I also bought some french wine for the fish I promised to cook.

sincerely

Sonya

Answers:

1A. Phil, go to the stock room and pick up the following: 4 boxes of M2-387, 2 boxes of D430Y, and 2 boxes of LDA73.

1B. OK

1C. You'll find them listed in the directory as Wilson, Thomas A.; Martin, Marcia L.; Thorndike, Robert C.; and Anthony, Susan D.

1D. Stop, thief!

1E. He looked in the cupboard for some crackers; there were none.

2. SONYA'S LETTER:

Dear Arthur:

Here is the box of Fine Fin Fish Food you asked me to pick up at the Foodway store on Lexington Avenue.

It costs so much to feed your hungry fish that I think you should say to them, "Swim south for the winter."

I also bought some French wine for the fish I promised to cook.

Sincerely,

Sonya

CHECK YOUR ANSWERS

1. Below are some sentences with direct and indirect quotations in them. Add or delete punctuation and capitalization to correct each example.

   A. harry said this was the right procedure.

   B. sylvia shouted we won we won

   C. well now martin said I don't believe
       we've had the pleasure of meeting.

   D. benjamin franklin statesman and inventor
       was lucky he wasn't killed flying his
       kite in that stormy philadelphia
       pennsylvania night

   E. in 1939 just 12 years after lindbergh's
       famous transatlantic flight douglas
       corrigan later called wrong way corrigan
       left new york city new york for long
       beach california but ended up in dublin
       ireland

   F. when asked about it corrigan told the
       officials I guess I accidentally flew the
       wrong way

2. In the next five questions, find the word in each set that is misspelled, if there is one. If there is no error, mark number ⑤.

   A. 1) conjunction
       2) semi-colon   2A. ① ② ③ ④ ⑤
       3) maintenance
       4) vocabulary
       5) no error

B. 1) apositive
    2) imperative
    3) renames
    4) university
    5) no error

2B. ① ② ③ ④ ⑤

C. 1) recieved
    2) clause
    3) phrase
    4) signature
    5) no error

2C. ① ② ③ ④ ⑤

D. 1) profile
    2) punctuation
    3) pronunciation
    4) capitalization
    5) no error

2D. ① ② ③ ④ ⑤

E. 1) historically
    2) nationalities
    3) discused
    4) chinaware
    5) no error

2E. ① ② ③ ④ ⑤

7. In the exercise below, you must be aware of spelling, punctuation, and capitalization. Write the corrections, additions, or deletions above the errors.

A. when phyllis standing on a ladder washing
    windowes fell she injured her back she
    experienced difficultys for weeks
    includeing triing to get out of bed
    walking upstairs even sitting on a
    straight chair

B. independence day our nation's birthday is
    also the aniversary of the death of three
    of our Presidents john adams and thomas
    jefferson both died july 4 1826 the

Quiz for Program 2 (continued)

```
        fiftyth anniversary of the adoption of

        the declaration of idependence our fifth

        president james monroe died july 4 1831
    C.  the adventures of huckleberry finn  is a

        novel by mark twain

    D.  who is at the door she asked

    E.  the night was dark shadows stood still
```

CHECK YOUR ANSWERS

Answers for the Quiz:

1A. Harry said this was the right procedure. (indirect quote)

1B. Sylvia shouted, "We won! we won!"

1C. "Well now," Martin said, "I don't believe we've had the pleasure of meeting."

1D. Benjamin Franklin, statesman and inventor, was lucky he wasn't killed flying his kite in that stormy Philadelphia, Pennsylvania, night.

1E. In 1939, just 12 years after Lindbergh's famous transatlantic flight, Douglas Corrigan, later called "Wrong Way Corrigan," left New York City, New York, for Long Beach, California, but ended up in Dublin, Ireland.

1F. When asked about it, Corrigan told the officials, "I guess I accidentally flew the wrong way."

2A. 5   2B. 1   2C. 1   2D. 5   2E. 3

7A. When Phyllis, standing on a ladder washing windows, fell, she injured her back. She experienced difficulties for weeks, including trying to get out of bed, walking upstairs, even sitting on a straight chair.

7B. Independence Day, our nation's birthday, is also the anniversary of the deaths of three of our presidents. John Adams and Thomas Jefferson both died July 4, 1826, the fiftieth anniversary of the adoption of the Declaration of Independence. Our fifth President, James Monroe, died July 4, 1831.

7C. *The Adventures of Huckleberry Finn* is a novel by Mark Twain.

7D. "Who is at the door?" she asked.

7E. The night was dark; shadows stood still.

Practice these words.

A. athletic	E. noticing	I. secretary
B. fourth	F. quiet	J. studying
C. forty	G. receive	K. truly
D. meant	H. similar	L. usually

SPELLING DEMONS

Special Demon

The word "occasion" is one of the most misspelled words in the English language. Memorize it!

Your Own List

On the lines below, continue to build your own word list. Remember to SEE-SAY-WRITE these words until they are a part of you.

_____   _____
_____   _____
_____   _____
_____   _____
_____

When You Write

Here's an exercise to help you put together some of the words we have studied into different written forms.

```
     the   the   quiet   tall   saw   president   general
```

These words can make sense only if you put them together in certain ways. For instance, you could write: "The tall general saw the quiet president."

On the lines below, see how many good sentences you can make, using all the words. Be sure to spell the words correctly.

_____
_____
_____
_____
_____
_____
_____
_____
_____
_____
_____
_____
_____

Answers:
The tall, quiet president saw the general.
The tall, quiet general saw the president.
The tall president saw the quiet general.
The tall general saw the quiet president.
The quiet general saw the tall president.
The quiet president saw the tall general.
The president saw the tall, quiet general.
The general saw the tall, quiet president.

CHECK YOUR
ANSWERS

Chapter
Three
Nouns &
Verbs

In this video, Arthur and Sonya attend a Shakespearean play. The implied connection to the study of nouns and verbs is that nouns are things of the world, such as actors, and verbs are what the actors do or what is done to them.

Sonya and Mrs. Johnson evaluate a speech from the play to find the way different types of nouns fit into the theme.

The discussion about the use of verbs and verb tense is an especially important scene.

Be alert.

Goal-Setting Exercise for Program 3

1. Find the errors in the sentences below. If there is an error, there will be only one. If there is no error in the sentence, mark answer number ⑤.

A. <u>Arthur and Sonya</u> <u>arrived</u> at the theatre   1A. ① ② ③ ④ ⑤
         ❶   ❷
    late and <u>seen</u> only the last half <u>of</u> the
              ❸   ❹
    play.   <u>no error</u>
                                            ❺

B. The committee <u>run</u> into trouble <u>trying</u> to   1B. ① ② ③ ④ ⑤
                  ❶   ❷
    <u>find a</u> solution to the <u>difficult</u> problem.
       ❸   ❹
                                     <u>no error</u>
                                        ❺

                                                        1C. ① ② ③ ④ ⑤

C. The weather signs <u>warns</u> us <u>that</u> an
                       ❶   ❷
    intensely <u>cold</u> winter <u>is</u> coming. <u>no error</u>
               ❸   ❹   ❺

D. A <u>flock</u> of pigeons <u>are</u> flying through the   1D. ① ② ③ ④ ⑤
       ❶   ❷
    <u>broken</u> windows of that <u>old</u> building.
       ❸   ❹
                                     <u>no error</u>
                                        ❺

2. Fill in the blank in each sentence with the correct form of the word choices listed.

A. I _____ to one of the biggest
       (went / have went)
    stores in town.

Goal-Setting Exercise for Program 3 (continued)

B. The team _____ going to a party.
                    (is / are)

C. Sonya _____ from Europe.
                   (come / came)

D. Arthur has _____ a good job on his
                     (did / done)
    book.

Answers for Goal-Setting Exercise:

1A. 3	1B. 1	1C. 1	1D. 2
2A. went	2B. is	2C. came	2D. done

CHECK YOUR ANSWERS

Viewing Prescription for Program 3

Put a check mark by each statement that is an accurate assessment of how you did.

❑ If you got them **all right** …

HURRAH! Evaluate Sonya's errors. Have you heard other people make these same mistakes?

❑ If you missed number **1A** …

pay close attention to the discussion of *tenses*.

❑ If you missed **1B**, **1C**, or **1D** …

number agreement is discussed in the video. Be alert.

❑ If you missed any of number **2** …

these are common *speaking errors*. Look at them again before you watch the video.

Vocabulary for Program 3

noun (NOWN) is a kind of word that is usually defined as "a person, place, or thing." This definition falls a little short, but it's a place to begin.

verb (VURB) is a word that shows an action relationship with the nouns and the other parts of a sentence. A verb can show what is called "a state of being." (More about that later.)

concrete (KAHN-kreet), when referring to a noun, means something real. For example: car, apple, man, woman, etc.

abstract (AB-strakt) is the opposite of concrete. In nouns, it refers to things you can't touch. Examples: love, trouble, patriotism, etc.

collective noun (coh-LECK-tiv) refers to a noun that is made up of parts but is thought of as a single unit. Examples: group, committee, population, etc.

compound noun (KAHM-pound) is a noun made up of two or more words that express a single thought. An example used in the video is musical comedy. Musical comedy is one thing, but it takes both words to express the idea.

state of being refers to verbs that don't show action but come between the noun and a word or phrase that tells about the main noun. This term is difficult to describe but easy to see in examples. (I am tall—"am" is a verb, even though it shows no action. It helps to tell about my "being.")

tense (TENSS) refers to that quality of verbs which allows you to know *when* something happened. Tense is what makes sentences "tell time." There are three major verb tenses: past, present, and future. All the others are forms of these three.

object (AHB-jekt) is a word that completes the meaning started by a subject and a verb. It answers the question "what" about a verb. *Example:* Arthur writes books. Arthur = subject; writes = verb; books = object (What does Arthur write? "books")
  Objects come in two types:
    A *direct object* answers the question "whom or what" about the verb.
      Arthur likes Sonya.
        (answers "whom")
      Arthur likes books.
        (answers "what")
    An *indirect object* answers the question "to whom or to what" or "for whom or for what" about the verb.
      Arthur gave Freddie a book.
        (answers "to whom")
      Arthur provided the fish some food.
        (answers "to what")

LEARN THE WORDS

Subject Matter Review: Nouns

Here are some of the main points of grammar covered in this program. It's a good idea to remember that some people spend a lifetime trying to learn all about English. In this short series, we can cover only some of the most important ideas.

What Nouns Do

Nouns act as the subjects of verbs.

The boys run.

The word boys is a noun and is the subject of the verb run.

Nouns act as direct objects.

The boys ran a race.

The word race is a noun and is the direct object of the verb ran. (ran what? a race)

NOTE: There are other ways for a noun to be an object. We'll talk about that later.

LEARN THE RULES

Noun Characteristics

Think of noun characteristics in pairs. Nouns can be:
common (city) or *proper* (Chicago)
concrete (apple) or- *abstract* (envy)
simple (sister) or *compound* (brother-in-law)
singular (cow) or *plural* (cows)
collective singular (herd) or *collective plural* (see explanation)

Nouns can be "concrete."

"As the curtain opened, the spotlight illuminated three witches cackling beneath the moon."

The underlined nouns are all CONCRETE because they name things that can be seen or touched.

Subject Matter Review: Nouns (continued)

Nouns can be "abstract."

"Some critics consider the <u>tension</u> between <u>power</u> and <u>honesty</u> to be the <u>theme</u> of *Macbeth*."

The underlined nouns refer to things that can not be seen or touched, so they are considered ABSTRACT.

Now practice identifying these two characteristics. In the sentences below, some of the nouns are underlined. Write "C" above those that are concrete and "A" above the abstract ones.

1. The <u>Declaration of Independence</u> was signed by a <u>group</u> of <u>men</u> whose <u>patriotism</u> goes unquestioned.

2. <u>Cells</u> in <u>plants</u> and <u>animals</u> are the basic units of <u>life</u>.

3. <u>Work</u> can be the <u>fulfillment</u> of a <u>person</u>'s entire <u>life</u>.

4. <u>Religion</u> is common to all <u>cultures</u>.

PRACTICE THE RULES

Answers:
1. Declaration of Independence—C; group—A; men—C; patriotism—A
2. Cells—C; plants—C; animals—C; life—A
3. Work—A; fulfillment—A; person—C; life—A
4. Religion—A; cultures—A

CHECK YOUR ANSWERS

Nouns can be "collective."

The video suggested the following collective nouns: <u>audience</u>, <u>crowd</u>, <u>group</u>, and <u>collection</u>. There are many others.

The jury is deliberating.

The word <u>jury</u> describes a group, and takes a singular verb.

But in this next sentence, the individual members of the jury are referred to, so the noun takes a plural verb.

LEARN THE RULE

Subject Matter Review: Nouns (continued)

The jury will call their families.

NOTE: Collective nouns are usually singular, but you must pay attention to the context.

Insert the proper collective nouns in the spaces in these sentences. Each noun is used only once.

Collectives to use: **band   association   tribe   group   herd**

1. The _____ of bison was stampeding

    toward the Indian _____ .

2. Steve had belonged to a rock _____

    before he joined the community

    _____ .

3. The merchants' _____ is planning a

    block party.

PRACTICE THE RULE

Answers:
1. herd, tribe
2. band, group
3. association

CHECK YOUR ANSWERS

Subject Matter Review: Verbs

Verbs show action—most of the time.

Some of the verbs used in the program that showed action were <u>write</u>, <u>run</u>, <u>begin</u>, <u>break</u>, <u>say</u> (and many, many more).

The form of the verb tells the time of a sentence: its "tense."

You can test the tense of the verb in a sentence by inserting the words today, yesterday, and tomorrow.

LEARN THE RULES

The boys <u>ran</u>.

What tense is the sentence in? (Today, the boys <u>run</u>. Yesterday the boys <u>ran</u>. Tomorrow the boys <u>will run</u>.) Notice that when you add <u>yesterday</u>, nothing else changes. This should tell you the original sentence was written in past tense—because it fits with <u>yesterday</u>, which is also in the past.

Sometimes verbs change tense by changing their endings.

Today the boy <u>walks</u> by the lake.
Yesterday the boy <u>walked</u> by the lake.
Tomorrow the boy <u>will walk</u> by the lake.
Today the boy <u>is walking</u> by the lake.

Verbs often need "helpers" to show time change.

Here is a list of the most common verb helpers.

is	were	could
am	are	would
was	do	should
be	does	may
been	did	might
being	have	must
was	has	shall
had	will	

Today the boy <u>is walking</u> by the lake.
Yesterday the boy <u>was walking</u> by the lake.

Irregular Verbs Have Irregular Forms.

The regular verbs change tense by simply adding "ed" or "d." The irregular verbs do not have this consistency. It's necessary to memorize them. Here is a partial list.

Base Form	Past Tense	Past Participle (used with helper)
be	was, were	been
begin	began	begun
break	broke	broken
bring	brought	brought
buy	bought	bought
choose	chose	chosen
come	came	come
do	did	done
drive	drove	driven
eat	ate	eaten

Subject Matter Review: Verbs (continued)

fight	fought	fought
find	found	found
forget	forgot	forgotten
forgive	forgave	forgiven
freeze	froze	frozen
go	went	gone
grow	grew	grown
know	knew	known
ride	rode	ridden
rise	rose	risen
run	ran	run
see	saw	seen
sing	sang	sung
speak	spoke	spoken
take	took	taken
throw	threw	thrown
wear	wore	worn
write	wrote	written

Cross out the incorrect verb in each sentence below.

1. Beverly (saw/seen) the bus coming.

2. If Anton (had ran/had run) better the last half of the race, he (would have/would of) won.

3. The scout troup (has/have) plans for a spring camp-out.

4. Stephanie's choir (is/are) giving a concert Saturday.

5. He (done/did) his best.

PRACTICE THE RULES

Answers:
1. saw   2. had run, would have   3. has
4. is   5. did

CHECK YOUR ANSWERS

Subject Matter Review: Verbs (continued)

Some verbs are "linking" verbs.

Think of a chain:

Alligators ◯ are ◯ reptiles.

LEARN THE RULES

Some verbs link the subject to other words in the sentence. Among the most common linking verbs:

is   was   am   are   be   been   were   being

The boy <u>is</u> tall.

Even some action verbs behave as linking verbs. Here is a partial list of such verbs which, in one form or another, serve as linking verbs.

seem   appear   remain   become   grow

… plus all the words that refer to the senses:

look   smell   taste   sound   feel

The boy <u>seemed</u> tall.

REMEMBER: You can test this kind of sentence because the other linking verbs can be substituted for them.

The boy <u>seemed</u> tall.	=	The boy <u>is</u> tall.
The girl <u>felt</u> hungry.	=	The girl <u>was</u> hungry.
They <u>appeared</u> lost.	=	They <u>were</u> lost.

In the sentences below, underline the linking verbs with a single line; action verbs with a double line.

1. Alex is tall, and when he swims, he cuts the water like a knife.

2. The horizon is only 20 miles away, but it appears much farther.

3. When a band is marching in a parade, it sends a chill up my spine.

4. When chili cooks on the stove, it smells so good.

PRACTICE THE RULES

Subject Matter Review: Verbs (continued)

CHECK YOUR ANSWERS

Answers:
1. is … swims … cuts
2. is … appears
3. is marching … sends
4. cooks … smells

LEARN THE RULES

Verbs have "voices."

Active voice: The subject does something.

Arthur wrote a book.

Passive voice: Something is done to the subject.

The book was written by Arthur.

These two elements will be more important in chapters to come for two reasons: You will be spending more time learning about subjects, and you will be writing more.

NOTE: You'll hear a lot about *agreement* in the next two chapters. This term refers to picking the right verb to fit the "number" of a noun and the "time" of the sentence.

Skill Helper

These pairs of verbs give many people a lot of trouble. Study these examples before you go on to the quiz.

SIT and SET

Sit means to sit down, to get into a chair or seat, or to remain seated.
   I sit today.
   I sat yesterday.
   I have sat many times.

Set means to place or put something down.
   Set the chair by the table.
   I set it there yesterday.
   I have set it there many times.

NOTE: Sit is never followed by an object. Set may be followed by an object. In the sentence "Set the chair by the table," chair is the object of set.

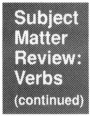

Subject Matter Review: Verbs (continued)

LIE and LAY

<u>Lie</u> means to lie down.
  I lie on the bed.
  Yesterday I lay on the bed.
  I have lain on this bed many times.

<u>Lay</u> means to put something down.
  Lay the book on the table.
  I laid it there yesterday.
  I have laid it there many times.

NOTE: These verbs are confusing because the past tense of <u>lie</u> is the same word as the present tense of <u>lay</u>. However, <u>lay</u> may have an object. <u>Lie</u> never does.

Also, the verb <u>lie</u>, which means to tell a falsehood, is another word entirely.

Quiz for Program 3

1. Underline all of the nouns in the next three sentences. Write "C" above each concrete one and "A" above each abstract one.

   A. When scientists talk about cells, they
       often mention the mitochondria, those
       little pieces of life that appear to
       belong to someone else.

   B. Greater understanding of the world around
       us has been a quest of man since the
       beginning of time.

   C. One of the most interesting creations on
       earth is the Portugese man-of-war. This
       member of the jellyfish family is not a
       single animal at all, but a colony of
       organisms, which live in such close
       proximity that they seem like one animal.

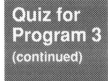

Quiz for Program 3 (continued)

2. In the sentences below, find what is wrong, if anything. If there is an error, decide which of the underlined parts must be changed to make it correct. If there is no error, mark number ⑤. No sentence has more than one error.

A. Early settlers <u>was</u> amazed that some of   2A. ① ② ③ ④ ⑤
                    ❶

the <u>Indian</u> words <u>sounded</u> like Gre<u>ek</u>.
        ❷   ❸   ❹

                                    <u>no error</u>
                                       ❺

B. Most scientists be<u>lieve</u> that the   2B. ① ② ③ ④ ⑤
                       ❶

<u>American Indians</u> <u>come</u> across a land
       ❷   ❸

bridge from Asi<u>a</u>.   <u>no error</u>
                ❹   ❺

C. When explorers first <u>seen</u> <u>Niagara Falls</u>,   2C. ① ② ③ ④ ⑤
                          ❶   ❷

they <u>were</u> surely <u>awe-inspired</u>.   <u>no error</u>
      ❸   ❹   ❺

3. Sonya wrote a letter in this video program. Below is a copy of the original, including all of her mistakes. First, underline the errors; then, in the space provided, rewrite the letter in correct form. An error may be in grammar, spelling, or punctuation.

Dear Mr. Lacy,

   In october sir I worked here for two

years. When I begun this job I just arrived

from Europe my homeland.

   I like my job very much. I worked hard. I

stay with your store. But I would like a

raise in salery.

Now write your version in the space below.

_____
_____
_____
_____
_____
_____
_____
_____
_____
_____
_____
_____

4. Circle the correct word choice in each of the following sentences.

    A. Correct posture is very important when
        (sitting/setting) on a straight chair.

    B. Just (sit/set) the boxes on that table.

    C. Please (lay/lie) still.

    D. (Lay/Lie) the boards there until we need
        them.

5. Here's another excerpt from the video. Circle the letter beside the
   changes that should be made from the list that follows.

        When it <u>begun</u> to thunde<u>r he</u> <u>was setting</u>
                    A   B   C

    peacefully in his chair. He <u>seen</u> it was going
                                  D

    to storm and he <u>walked</u> over to close the
                       E

    windows he had <u>risen</u> earlier. He wondered
                      F

    if he <u>had brung</u> in the newspaper<u>. because</u> he
             G   H

    <u>knowed</u> it <u>will</u> be raining soon.
       I   J

Quiz for
Program 3
(continued)

A. 1) change <u>begun</u> to <u>had begun</u>
    2) change <u>begun</u> to <u>began</u>
    3) no error

B. 1) put a period after <u>thunder</u>;
        capitalize <u>he</u>
    2) put a comma after <u>thunder</u>
    3) no error

C. 1) change <u>was setting</u> to <u>had been set-</u>
        <u>ting</u>
    2) change <u>setting</u> to <u>sitting</u>
    3) no error

D. 1) change <u>seen</u> to <u>had seen</u>
    2) change <u>seen</u> to <u>saw</u>
    3) no error

E. 1) change <u>walked</u> to <u>is walking</u>
    2) change <u>walked</u> to <u>had walked</u>
    3) no error

F. 1) change <u>risen</u> to <u>raised</u>
    2) change <u>risen</u> to <u>rose</u>
    3) no error

G. 1) change <u>had brung</u> to <u>brung</u>
    2) change <u>had brung</u> to <u>had brought</u>
    3) no error

H. 1) remove period after <u>newspaper</u>
    2) insert comma after <u>newspaper</u>
    3) no error

I. 1) change <u>knowed</u> to <u>knew</u>
    2) change <u>knowed</u> to <u>had knowed</u>
    3) no error

J. 1) change <u>will</u> to <u>would</u>
    2) change <u>will</u> to <u>was</u>; omit <u>be</u>
    3) no error

Quiz for Program 3 (continued)

Answers for Quiz:

1A. CONCRETE: scientists, cells, mitochondria, pieces, someone else
ABSTRACT: life

1B. CONCRETE: world, man
ABSTRACT: understanding, quest, beginning, time

1C. CONCRETE: earth, Portugese man-of-war, member, jelly fish family, animals, colony, organisms
ABSTRACT: creations, proximity

2A. 1   2B. 3   2C. 1

3. Dear Mr. Lacy:

    In October, sir, I will have worked here for two years. When I began this job, I had just arrived from Europe, my homeland.

    I like my job very much. I have worked hard. I will stay with your store, but I would like a raise in salary.

4A. sitting   4B. set   4C. lie   4D. lay

5A. 2   5B. 2   5C. 2   5D. 2   5E. 3

5F. 1   5G. 2   5H. 2   5I. 1   5J. 1

CHECK YOUR ANSWERS

Practice these words.

A. acquaint	E. finally	I. surprise
B. boundary	F. government	J. twelfth
C. business	G. library	
D. February	H. recognize	

SPELLING DEMONS

On these words, the SAY step is the important one. Many people leave out some of the sounds in these words; therefore, they misspell them.

Special Demon

The word INTERESTING is another one of the frequently misspelled words because we mispronounce it. This word has four syllables:

IN-TER-EST-ING.

Your Own List

Continue building your own list. Go back through this chapter and find words you might have difficulty with. SEE them, SAY them, and WRITE them on the lines below.

_____   _____

_____   _____

_____   _____

_____   _____

_____   _____

When You Write

It's time for you to start building sentences. This lesson was about nouns and verbs, the two essential ingredients of a sentence. Write five sentences in which the subject does the acting. Then write five more in which the subject is acted upon.

Examples:

Harry opened the gate. (Harry does the acting.)

The gate was opened by Harry. (Gate is the subject, but it receives the action.)

_____

_____

_____

_____

_____

_____

_____

_____

_____

_____

_____

_____

_____

Chapter
Four
Agreement

You expect Arthur to be writing because that's what he does for a living. But in this program, it seems, *everybody* is writing something.

You will be introduced to the wonderful world of subject-verb agreement. First, you'll see how to find the subject of a sentence, or what the sentence is about. Then, you'll see how to decide which verb form should be used with the subject.

This program is important if you need to improve your ability to write.

Once you understand how the subject and verb work together, writing (as Freddy finds out) becomes much easier.

As you watch the program, see if you can identify those things that cause you problems when you write.

It would be a good idea to go back to chapters two and three and review the vocabulary sections. Vocabulary accumulates. You will be hearing words that were used in those two chapters.

Goal-Setting Exercise for Program 4

In the sentences below, circle the correct forms of the verbs.

1. Sam (walk / walks) to the bus stop.

2. Neither the train nor the truck (was / were) big enough to haul all the grain.

3. Ham, eggs and grits (is / are) my favorite meal.

4. Only horses and carriages (is / are) allowed on the island.

5. Each of the four ideas (has / have) some good points.

6. A Tale of Two Cities (are / is) exciting.

7. He wanted to know if there (was / were) any news.

8. None of the soldiers (was / were) injured.

9. You (was / were) supposed to be here when the guests arrived.

10. The number of people on a train (don't / doesn't) affect its speed.

11. Not only the book shelves but also the cupboard (was / were) full of books.

Answers for Goal-Setting Exercise:

1. walks	2. was	3. is	4. are	5. has
6. is	7. was	8. was	9. were	10. doesn't
11. was				

CHECK YOUR ANSWERS

Viewing Prescription for Program 4

Put a check mark by each statement that is an accurate assessment of how you did.

❑ If you got them **all right** …

you're very AGREEABLE. Pay attention to how Arthur and Freddy go about organizing the maintenance manual.

❑ If you missed number **1** …

listen to the discussion of ***plural and singular subjects***.

❑ If you missed number **2** …

this is a special case, which is discussed in the video.

❑ If you missed number **3 or 4** …

these two examples sound the same, but they aren't. Arthur explains the difference.

❑ If you missed number **5** …

you may need more practice in ***identifying the subject*** of a sentence. Arthur and Freddy can be of help.

❑ If you missed number **6** …

titles and the like are special cases, too. Pay close attention to the discussion in the video.

❑ If you missed number **7** …

some words end in "s" but are singular. What does Arthur say about mumps?

❑ If you missed number **8** …

be careful of sentences like this one. What rule is in the video about ***none, either/or, neither/nor***?

❑ If you missed number **9** …

this is a common error. Be sure you complete ALL the exercises in the practice section of this chapter.

❑ If you missed number **10** …

numbers need special treatment.

❑ If you missed number **11** …

this type of sentence is discussed in the video and the exercises that follow the program.

Vocabulary for Program 4

subject (SUB-jekt) is the "actor" of the sentence. Find the verb, then ask, "Who or what is performing the action?" Here's an example:

The boy ran.

The verb is ran; it shows action. If you ask, "Who ran?", your answer is "The boy." Therefore, boy is the subject of the sentence. While this is a simple sentence, the same trick works on more complicated ones.

clause (KLAWS) refers to a group of words that go together in a sentence but do not constitute a sentence by themselves. Clauses must have subjects and verbs in them. For example:

That is the woman who drove the car.

The underlined portion is the clause. The subject of the clause is who, and the verb is drove. The subject of this sentence, however, is woman. The clause just tells more about the woman.

phrase (FRAZE) refers to another kind of word grouping in a sentence. Phrases behave as if they were single words. They are different from clauses because they do not have subjects and verbs.

number refers to the quality of words that allows them to talk about one or more things. You will hear, "Subjects and verbs must agree in number." Nouns that refer to more than one thing must have verbs that do the same.

LEARN THE WORDS

NOW WATCH PROGRAM 4

Subject Matter Review

*This section contains rules for **subject-verb agreement**.*

The main points covered in this program have to do with sentence structure in which the subject and the verb are in agreement; that is, they are "right for each other." You noticed that the forms of the verbs change according to whether their subjects are plural or singular.

The subject of a sentence is a noun or a noun substitute. (We'll talk about these substitutes later.) Nouns may be singular or plural in number. A verb must agree in number with its subject.

LEARN THE RULES

Singular subjects use singular verbs; plural subjects must have plural verbs.

> One bus <u>is</u> parked outside.
> Forty passengers <u>are</u> on the bus.
> One apple <u>costs</u> 20 cents.
> Two apples <u>cost</u> 40 cents.

A compound subject requires a plural verb.

> Apples and oranges <u>are</u> expensive
> The apples and oranges <u>are</u> expensive.

With either/or and neither/nor, a singular verb is used when both nouns are singular. When a singular and plural noun are in a compound subject, *the verb takes the form of the noun closer to the verb.*

> Either Arthur or Sonya <u>is</u> going.
> Neither Arthur nor Sonya <u>is</u> going.
> Either the driver or the passengers <u>are</u> going.
> Either the passengers or the driver <u>is</u> going.
> *(<u>Driver</u> is closer to the verb, so use the singular form.)*

A collective noun takes a singular verb when the group acts as a unit and a plural verb when the members of the group act as individuals.

> The team <u>plays</u> next Saturday.
> The faculty <u>disagree</u> about the best teaching strategy.
> (This means "The *members of the faculty* disagree.")

Nouns that have plural forms but singular meanings use singular verbs.

> Physics <u>is</u> a difficult subject.

Subject
Matter
Review
(continued)

Numbers, quantities, sums of money, and periods of time use singular verbs.

Two weeks <u>is</u> a long time to wait.
Fifty dollars <u>is</u> too much to pay.

A fraction takes a singular verb if it refers to a value that is less than one or can't be counted.

Two-thirds of the food <u>has</u> been eaten.
Three-fourths of the accidents <u>were</u> caused by drunken driving.

Subjects that include <u>each</u>, <u>every</u>, <u>anybody</u>, <u>nobody</u>, <u>none</u>, <u>anything</u>, <u>no one</u>, <u>someone</u>, <u>everyone</u>, or <u>everybody</u> use singular verbs.

Everybody <u>is</u> allowed the same opportunity.

If <u>all</u>, <u>any</u>, <u>more</u>, <u>most</u>, <u>some</u>, <u>that</u>, <u>what</u>, <u>who</u>, or <u>which</u> is the subject, whether the verb is singular or plural depends on what the rest of the sentence implies. If it implies a single unit, use a singular verb. If, however, it has a plural sense, use the plural form.

Most of the money <u>was</u> stolen.
   (Money is a quantity.)
Most of the cows <u>were</u> stolen.
   (This has a plural sense.)
None <u>was</u> forgotten.

Special Cases

There, Here

In a sentence beginning with <u>there is</u> or <u>there are</u> (or <u>here is</u>, or <u>here are</u>), the implied sense of the rest of the sentence determines the form of the verb. Remember, <u>there</u> or <u>here</u> will never be the subject of this type of sentence. Look for the subject after the <u>there</u> or <u>here</u> phrase.

There <u>is</u> a dent in each fender.
   (The subject, <u>dent</u>, uses <u>is</u>.)
There <u>are</u> dents in other places, too.
   (<u>Dents</u> is plural and uses <u>are</u>.)

Number

If a sentence says "THE number …," use a singular verb.

The number of smallpox cases <u>decreases</u> each year.

Subject Matter Review (continued)

If a sentence says "A number …," use a plural verb.

A number of cases <u>are</u> still reported, nevertheless.

"If …"

People frequently use an incorrect verb form in the following situations. "If I (was/were) you … " The correct form is always <u>were</u>: "If I <u>were</u> you …,"You <u>were</u> supposed to …," "I thought you <u>were</u> going to …" and so forth. Never use <u>was</u> in sentences that fit the above patterns.

Grammar Tip

If you have trouble with a particular rule, find a model sentence you can remember that applies the rule. When you have a question about correct form, substitute the parts of the sentence in question for the parts in your model.

Suppose you have trouble using <u>every</u>. Use this sentence as a model: "<u>Every</u> good boy <u>does</u> fine." Now look at this sentence.

<u>Every</u> nail in the box (was / were) bent.

<u>Was</u> is the correct choice, because it is a singular verb and so is <u>does</u>. There may be many nails in the box, but <u>every</u> tells you to use a singular verb.

1. In the sentences below, find the errors in agreement and correct them. If there is no error in a sentence, place a "C" above the underlined verb. Several of the sentences have correct subject-verb agreement.

   A. There<u>'s</u> your tickets on the table.

   B. Jim's house and barn <u>has</u> been painted every year for as long as I can remember.

   C. Mathematics <u>has</u> always been easy for me.

   D. Either several workers or their supervisor <u>inspects</u> the elevator each morning.

   E. Do you think 50 dollars <u>are</u> enough to buy what we need?

   F. The number of accidents due to drunken driving <u>have</u> decreased.

PRACTICE THE RULES

G. A committee of seven people <u>were</u> studying the problem.

H. George Washington, as well as many other Revolutionary War heroes, <u>has</u> a special place in our history.

2. Fill in each blank with the correct form of the verb below it. Remember: If a collective noun is considered as a group, then a singular verb is used. If, however, the sentence is written so that you think of the individuals of that group, use a plural verb.

A. The committee _____ a change
                  [recommend]
in policy.

B. The Congress _____ in session
             [is]
at this time.

C. It was late, so the jury _____
                [was]
asked to order their dinners.

D. The Board of Directors _____
              [was]
meeting, but the members _____
              [was]
arguing over a point of order.

E. The number of lost children _____
             [is]
surprisingly large.

F. A majority of these children

_____ never found.
  [is]

G. All _____ been lost.
     [has]

H. Most of the work _____ been
            [has]
done.

Subject Matter Review (continued)

I. None of the apples _____ ripe.
                                [was]

J. This beer _____ few calories.
                    [contain]

Answers:

1A. There are	1B. have	1C. C
1D. C	1E. is	1F. has
1G. was	1H. C	2A. recommends
2B. is	2C. were	2D. was, were
2E. is	2F. are	2G. has or have
		(depends on context)
2H. has	2I. was	2J. contains

CHECK YOUR ANSWERS

A Different Kind of Subject

You know that nouns can be subjects, BUT some noun substitutes also can be subjects.

For instance, you could say "Bill went to town." <u>Bill</u> is the subject, and <u>went</u> is the verb. However, you might say instead, "He went to town." In this sentence, <u>He</u> is the subject, substituting for <u>Bill</u>.

<u>He</u> is a pronoun. It is a special type of pronoun that can serve as the subject of a sentence. Not all pronouns can be subjects, but that's the topic for the next chapter.

LEARN THE RULE

Here are some sentences with pronouns that can be subjects. In each blank, write a verb that makes sense in the sentence. Use the correct form.

1. I _____ currently attending college at a

   liberal arts school.

2. He _____ now running for chairman.

3. They _____ a mysterious group of people.

4. You _____ expected to attend the ceremony.

5. She _____ a very capable person.

PRACTICE THE RULE

Answers:

   1. am   2. is   3. are   4. are   5. is

CHECK YOUR ANSWERS

Verbs Must Agree about Time.

If a sentence has more than one verb, their tenses must agree.

Arthur <u>will write</u> the book and Sonya <u>reads</u> it.

This sentence is incorrect because <u>will write</u> is a different tense from <u>reads</u>. This sentence should say:

Arthur <u>writes</u> the book and Sonya <u>reads</u> it.

   - or -

Arthur <u>will write</u> the book and Sonya <u>will read</u> it.

LEARN THE RULES

In these exercises, write the forms of the underlined verbs that are consistent with the other verbs in the sentences.

1. The trucker parked his truck, and the

   warehouse crew <u>unloads</u> it.

2. When Steve found the treasure, he <u>gives</u> it to

   the museum.

3. The tree fell in the storm but <u>misses</u> the

   house.

PRACTICE THE RULES

Answers:

  1. unloaded   2. gave   3. missed

CHECK YOUR ANSWERS

Quiz for Program 4

1. Errors in the sentences below may be in spelling, capitalization, punctuation, or subject-verb agreement. Find the error, if there is one, and mark its number. If there is no error, mark number ⑤. No sentence has more than one error.

A. One of the most <u>beautiful trees</u>, the   1A. ① ② ③ ④ ⑤
                        ❶

    <u>american elm</u>, <u>has been</u> attacked by a
      ❷   ❸

    severe <u>disease</u>.   <u>no error</u>
        ❹   ⑤

B. The <u>disease</u> <u>is</u> so widespread that it   1B. ① ② ③ ④ ⑤
       ❶   ❷

    <u>has killed</u> all of the American elm trees
      ❸

    in some places in the <u>country</u>.   <u>no error</u>
                      ❹   ⑤

C. A beetle<u>, the Scolytus,</u> <u>carries</u> a disease- 1C. ① ② ③ ④ ⑤
         ❶   ❷

    causing <u>fungus</u> from <u>tree to tree</u>. <u>no error</u>
        ❸   ❹   ⑤

D. The <u>beetle</u> and the <u>fungus</u> together <u>causes</u> 1D. ① ② ③ ④ ⑤
      ❶   ❷   ❸

    the trees to <u>die</u>.   <u>no error</u>
            ❹   ⑤

E. Scientists think the <u>Dutch elm disease</u>,   1E. ① ② ③ ④ ⑤
                  ❶

    <u>as it is called,</u> <u>was imported</u> from <u>europe</u>
      ❷   ❸   ❹

    in a shipload of burl.   <u>no error</u>
                           ⑤

Quiz for Program 4 (continued)

F. Some <u>cities</u> and towns <u>has enacted</u> laws   1F. ① ② ③ ④ ⑤
   ❶   ❷

 for the <u>protection</u> of their <u>elms</u>. <u>no error</u>
        ❸   ❹   ❺

G. The <u>number</u> of living trees <u>have declined</u>   1G. ① ② ③ ④ ⑤
     ❶   ❷

 <u>dramatically</u> since the disease <u>started</u> to
     ❸   ❹

 spread.   <u>no error</u>
                            ❺

H. As soon as the disease <u>is detected</u>,   1H. ① ② ③ ④ ⑤
                  ❶

 <u>infected</u> trees must <u>be cut</u> and <u>burn</u>.
  ❷   ❸   ❹

                        <u>no error</u>
                            ❺

I. Neither sprays <u>nor</u> fertilizer <u>have been</u>   1I. ① ② ③ ④ ⑤
            ❶   ❷

 able to <u>deter</u> the <u>spread</u> of the disease.
       ❸   ❹

                        <u>no error</u>
                            ❺

J. In some <u>states</u>, the   1J. ① ② ③ ④ ⑤
       ❶

 <u>department of natural resources</u> <u>has thrown</u>
             ❷   ❸

 a major part of its <u>efforts</u> into
               ❹

 discovering a cure.   <u>no error</u>
                        ❺

K. <u>Each</u> tree that <u>becomes infected</u> <u>spreads</u>   1K. ① ② ③ ④ ⑤
  ❶   ❷   ❸

 the disease to nearby <u>healthy</u> trees.
               ❹

                        <u>no error</u>
                            ❺

L. One of the <u>difficulties</u> in solving the   1L. ① ② ③ ④ ⑤
                      ❶

problem <u>have been</u> the tendency one <u>elm</u>
              ❷   ❸

has to graft itself to <u>others</u> close by.
                              ❹

                                      <u>no error</u>
                                          ❺

M. Most <u>of the trees</u> that <u>have died</u> in   1M. ① ② ③ ④ ⑤
              ❶   ❷

<u>cities</u> <u>have been</u> cut down.   <u>no error</u>
    ❸   ❹   ❺

N. <u>Foresters</u> and environmentalists <u>agrees</u>   1N. ① ② ③ ④ ⑤
    ❶   ❷

that the <u>situation</u> is <u>critical</u>.   <u>no error</u>
              ❸   ❹   ❺

O. A number <u>of trees</u> <u>were</u> cut in   1O. ① ② ③ ④ ⑤
                  ❶   ❷

<u>Springfield, Illinois</u>, and all of their
          ❸

roots <u>were</u> destroyed.   <u>no error</u>
        ❹   ❺

2. A part of each sentence is underlined. This underlined portion may or
   may not contain an error. Mark the number of the change that would
   make the sentence correct; or, mark ⑤ if there is no error.

A. The <u>citizens and the town board meet</u> in   2A. ① ② ③ ④ ⑤
    this room tomorrow.
    1) citizens and town board meet
    2) citizens and Town Board meets
    3) citizens and Town Board met
    4) citizens and the Town Board will meet
    5) no change

Quiz for Program 4 (continued)

B. <u>There is many</u> items of business on the agenda.   2B. ① ② ③ ④ ⑤
1) There is lots
2) There are many
3) Here are many
4) There was many
5) no change

C. One question is whether <u>$5,000 are too much</u> to spend on street repair.   2C. ① ② ③ ④ ⑤
1) $5,000 is too much
2) $5,000 are too little
3) five thousand dollars are too much
4) Five Thousand Dollars is enough
5) no change

D. The <u>president of the Board</u> also owns the local grocery.   2D. ① ② ③ ④ ⑤
1) board President
2) Board President
3) president of the Town Board
4) President of the Board
5) no errors

E. A majority of the <u>citizens vote</u> for the Town Board members last November.   2E. ① ② ③ ④ ⑤
1) citizens votes
2) citizens voted
3) citizens will vote
4) citizens should vote
5) no change

F. The Board Treasurer will read the financial report and the <u>secretary took notes</u>.   2F. ① ② ③ ④ ⑤
1) Secretary will take notes
2) Secretary took notes
3) secretary takes notes
4) Secretary take notes
5) no change

Quiz for Program 4
(continued)

3. In each set of words below, find the misspelled word, if there is one. No set has more than one misspelling. If all the words are correct, mark ⑤.

A. 1) athaletic
    2) meant
    3) studying
    4) truly
    5) no error   3A. ① ② ③ ④ ⑤

B. 1) usually
    2) noticing
    3) receive
    4) fourth
    5) no error   3B. ① ② ③ ④ ⑤

C. 1) acquaint
    2) government
    3) business
    4) boundry
    5) no error   3C. ① ② ③ ④ ⑤

D. 1) completely
    2) sincerely
    3) corageous
    4) enabling
    5) no error   3D. ① ② ③ ④ ⑤

E. 1) worrying
    2) forrest
    3) carefully
    4) puppies
    5) no error   3E. ① ② ③ ④ ⑤

F. 1) irregular
    2) illegal
    3) inferring
    4) statement
    5) no error   3F. ① ② ③ ④ ⑤

**Quiz for
Program 4
(continued)**

G. 1) piece
    2) wierd
    3) forfeit
    4) their
    5) no error

3G. ① ② ③ ④ ⑤

H. 1) agreeable
    2) desirable
    3) tomatos
    4) accidental
    5) no error

3H. ① ② ③ ④ ⑤

I. 1) companies
    2) busyly
    3) uneasiness
    4) coming
    5) no error

3I. ① ② ③ ④ ⑤

Answers for Quiz:

1A. 2	1B. 5	1C. 5	1D. 3	1E. 4
1F. 2	1G. 2	1H. 4	1I. 2	1J. 2
1K. 5	1L. 2	1M. 5	1N. 2	1O. 5
2A. 4	2B. 2	2C. 1	2D. 2	2E. 2
2F. 1	3A. 1	3B. 5	3C. 4	3D. 3
3E. 2	3F. 5	3G. 2	3H. 3	3I. 2

**CHECK YOUR
ANSWERS**

**SPELLING
DEMONS**

O.K., you say that you SEE-SAY-WRITE every word you see and you still have difficulty learning to spell a list of words correctly?

Use this plan for a while: SEE-SAY-WRITE-*FEEL*-WRITE AGAIN. To FEEL a word, trace the word with your finger on something that feels pleasant to you. Many people like the feel of velvet or some other soft cloth.

From now on, SEE the word. SAY the word, being sure to pronounce every syllable. WRITE the word. FEEL the word. Trace it several times with your finger. Write it in the air. Write it on your forehead. Then write it again on paper.

Use this new plan on the demons in this lesson.

A. knowledge	F. scene	K. parallel
B. immediately	G. toward	L. personnel
C. pleasant	H. restaurant	M. scissors
D. thorough	I. regrettable	N. sergeant
E. receive	J. pamphlet	O. physician

Special Demon

OCCURRED is often misspelled. Try the new plan. SEE-SAY-WRITE-FEEL-WRITE AGAIN. If that doesn't work, memorize it.

Your Own List

Don't forget that your own list should include difficult words you find in your everyday life. The next time you read the want ads in the newspaper, see if you find words that should be included here.

_____   _____
_____   _____
_____   _____
_____   _____
_____   _____

When You Write

In this chapter, we've talked about simple subject-verb agreement. We haven't said much about the kinds of verbs you choose. When you write, the verbs you use should be colorful and express exactly the action you want to show. You'll find that what you write is less boring, too. Below is an exercise to help you see how different something sounds when you give special attention to verb selection.

Examples:
   Martha <u>hit</u> the mosquito.
   Martha <u>squashed</u> the mosquito.

See the difference? The sentences both say the same thing, but the second one is more vivid.

In the exercise below, select the verb(s) you like best in each sentence and write it in the blank above. If you can think of even better ones, use them.

1. The break dancers _____ in the
                [danced / spun / gyrated / talked]
   courthouse square.

2. As the music _____ from the,
                [came / blared / poured / whined]
   speakers, the activity _____ to
                        [grew / sprang / swelled / heaved]
   a fever pitch.

3. Passersby were _____ by the
                [impressed / captivated / intrigued / enthralled]
   vigorous gymnastics of the young people.

4. Looking more like robots than humans, the

   sidewalk entertainers _____
                                [went / spun / whirled / flew]
   through their routines.

Chapter
Five
Pronouns

Sonya gets a chance to fill in for Mrs. Johnson. She soon discovers that summarizing a stack of reports is an overwhelming job. She gets a little relief from the task when she has to write a report of an exciting incident involving Freddy, an elevator, and a pregnant woman.

Arthur offers some excellent advice, not only for solving problems with pronouns, but also for tackling any job that seems impossible.

Learning the proper use of pronouns isn't an impossible job. It will be a lot easier after this lesson.

Goal-Setting Exercise for Program 5

Answer these questions and follow the instructions in the viewing prescription.

In this exercise, circle the correct form for each word in the parentheses.

1. (He / Him) went to meet (she / her).

2. (He and she / Him and her) (live / lives) in Chicago.

3. (They / Them) (are / is) afraid of the storm.

4. Give the book to (she / her).

5. (He / Him) went to speak with (she / her).

6. (They / /Them), (who / which) were in the lifeboat, called to (we / us).

7. (He / Him) and (I / me) went with (she / her) and (they / them).

8. (I / Me) am taller than (he / him).

9. You are supposed to give the box to (they / them).

10. (They / Them) gave gifts to (we / us) graduating students.

Answers:

1. He, her	2. He and she, live	3. They, are
4. her	5. He, her	6. They, who, us
7. He, I, her, them	8. I, he	9. them
10. They, us		

CHECK YOUR ANSWERS

Viewing Prescription for Program 5

Check your answers, and then find your prescription for viewing by putting a check by each statement that applies.

❏ If you got them **all right** ...

Can you believe how well you're doing? See how many times Arthur refers to the relationship between prepositions and pronouns. What Arthur says on the telephone is very important.

❏ If you missed number **1** ...

Arthur will give you some help with this. Also, many examples are in this chapter.

❏ If you missed number **2** or **3** ...

Arthur mentions several times how certain kinds of *verbs* affect the choice of pronouns. Be alert.

❏ If you missed **4, 5, 7,** or **9** ...

Arthur tells several ways you can answer questions like this. Pay particular attention to the pronouns that can be *subjects* and those that can be *objects*.

❏ If you missed number **6** ...

listen carefully to what is said about *"who"* and *"which"* in the program.

❏ If you missed number **8** ...

what do the *"state of being"* verbs have to do with pronouns?

❏ If you missed number **10** ...

the workbook exercises can help you.

Vocabulary for Program 5

LEARN THE WORDS

antecedent (an-tuh-SEE-dunt) is the word in a sentence that a pronoun refers to. Pronouns must always "agree" with their antecedents.

pronoun (PROH-noun) is a noun substitute.

Pronoun-subject is a pronoun that can be the subject of the verb in a sentence.

Pronoun-object is a pronoun that can be an object. Not all of them can.

Pronoun-possessive is a pronoun that shows ownership.
   Mary put on her coat. (The coat belongs to Mary.)

number refers to singular or plural (one or more than one).

gender (JEN-dur) can be "masculine" (he), "feminine" (she), or "neuter" (it). A pronoun must always agree with the gender of its antecendent.

NOTE: English is a changing language. Once, it was correct to use the masculine pronoun when the antecedent's gender was unknown.

   Everyone lost <u>his</u> way.

This is no longer true. The form being accepted more and more in sentences such as the one above is "his or her."

NOW
WATCH
PROGRAM
5

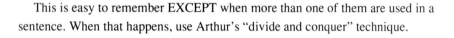

Subject Matter Review

Here are the main rules about pronouns. Practice each type.

Pronouns can be subjects.

The pronoun-subject of a sentence must be one of these pronouns:

I   you   he   she   it   we   they   who

This is easy to remember EXCEPT when more than one of them are used in a sentence. When that happens, use Arthur's "divide and conquer" technique.

William and (she / her) went to the movies.

This sentence means William went to the movies and she went to the movies. You wouldn't say, "Her went to the movies."

Circle the correct forms.

1. (Who / Whom) was elected president?

2. Sally and (her / she) are good friends.

3. (He / Him), (she / her) and (I / me) traveled together in Spain.

4. Because of the fire, (they / them) left the area.

Answers:
1. Who
3. He, she, I
2. she
4. they

LEARN THE RULES

PRACTICE THE RULES

CHECK YOUR ANSWERS

Pronouns can be objects.

If a pronoun is an object, use one of these:

me   you   him   her   it   us   them   whom

A good check of a pronoun-object is to put TO before the word, and see how it sounds:

to me   to you   to him   to her   to it   to us   to them   to whom

These sound OK. It would sound funny to say "to I."

In its objective form, a pronoun can be used as a direct object or an indirect object. Pronouns often are used as the objects of prepositions. Here are some examples.

We saw Billy and (he / <u>him</u>) at the station. (direct object)
Billy gave (I / <u>me</u>) and (she / <u>her</u>) a poster. (indirect objects)
The poster was given to (I / <u>me</u>) and (she / <u>her</u>). (objects of the preposition <u>to</u>)
I got it from (he / <u>him</u>). (object of the preposition <u>from</u>)
Just between you and (I / <u>me</u>) ... (object of the preposition <u>between</u>)

Here is a list of common prepositions.

about	before	during	off	under
above	behind	except	on	underneath
across	below	for	over	until
after	beneath	from	past	onto
against	beside	in	since	up
along	between	into	through	upon
among	beyond	like	throughout	with
around	by	near	to	within
at	down	of	toward	without

LEARN THE RULES

Circle the correct forms.

1. They elected (who / whom)?

2. Sally is a good friend to (her / she).

3. They traveled to Spain with (her / she) and
   (I / me).

PRACTICE THE RULES

Subject Matter Review (continued)

4. The fire forced (they / them) to leave.

5. Bill sold (I / me) a lemon of a car.

6. Marcellus told (them / they) a wild tale.

Answers:
  1. whom   2. her   3. her, me
  4. them   5. me   6. them

CHECK YOUR ANSWERS

Pronouns can show possession.

This little chart shows the subject, object, and possession forms of some nouns and pronouns. Notice that the nouns don't change very much, but the pronouns do.

Subject Form	Object Form	Possession Form
chair	chair	chair's
it	it	its*
Amanda	Amanda	Amanda's
she	her	her or hers*
players	players	players'
they	them	their or theirs*

LEARN THE RULES

* Notice that pronoun-possessives DO NOT use apostrophes.

WARNING: Be careful of pronoun "sound-alikes."

Possessive	Sound-Alike
its	it's (contraction for "it is")
whose	who's (contraction for "who is")
their	they're (contraction for "they are")
theirs	there's (contraction for "there is")

Circle the correct forms.

1. The dog licked (its / it's) paw.

2. The committee made (their / its) decision.

PRACTICE THE RULES

Subject Matter Review (continued)

3. The committee members ate (their / its) lunches.

4. Our neighbors lost (their / there) dog.

5. We went to the concert by (ourself / ourselves).

Answers:
1. its   2. its   3. their   4. their   5. ourselves

CHECK YOUR ANSWERS

If a pronoun is used as an appositive, use the same form (subject or object) for the pronoun as the word the appositive explains.

I talked to two pilots, Fred and him.

This sentence means: "I talked to Fred and I talked to him."

LEARN THE RULES

Circle the correct forms.

1. The two pilots, Fred and (he / him), wore new uniforms.

2. Bill called for the lifeguards, Marie and (she / her).

3. Martha's friend, Joe, and (her / she) went to the department store.

PRACTICE THE RULES

Answers:
1. he   2. her   3. she

CHECK YOUR ANSWERS

Subject Matter Review (continued)

After a linking verb, you must use a subject pronoun:

I   you   she   it   we   they   who

The people in the car <u>are</u> Arthur and <u>she</u>.

Remember Arthur's telephone conversation.

"This is he." (pronoun-subject)

When the sentence is a comparison, the same rule applies.

He is smarter than I.

You can check this out by adding another verb to the end of a sentence.

He is smarter than <u>I</u> am. (correct)
He is smarter than <u>me</u> am. (incorrect)

Circle the correct forms.

1. It is (he / him) (who / whom) locks the door at night.

2. The winner is (whoever / whomever) crosses the finish line first.

3. I think Sarah is prettier than (she / her).

4. I know it was (he / him).

5. You can bet your life it was (they / them).

Answers:

1. he, who
2. whoever
3. she
4. he
5. they

LEARN THE RULES

PRACTICE THE RULES

CHECK YOUR ANSWERS

Subject Matter Review (continued)

Pronouns must agree in more than one way with their antecedents.

They must agree in number:

Singular—   Everything <u>was</u> in its place.
Plural—   All things <u>were</u> in their places.

They must agree in gender:

Feminine—   Sally was in <u>her</u> seat.
Masculine—   Robert hurt <u>his</u> hand.
Neuter—   The tree lost <u>its</u> leaves.

LEARN THE RULES

Circle the correct forms.

1. The race cars lost (their / its) wheels.

2. Arthur and Sonya seated (himself or herself / themselves).

3. He found the bicycle, but both (its / their) tires were missing.

PRACTICE THE RULES

Answers:
1. their   2. themselves   3. its

```
NEVER NEVER NEVER NEVER NEVER NEVER
hisself    -or-    theirself
```

CHECK YOUR ANSWERS

Now for some mixed practice: These sentences may require any of the types of pronoun forms you've studied. Circle the correct forms.

1. Everybody learned (their / his / his or her) lesson.

2. The delivery men brought chairs, and (he or she / they) arranged them in the auditorium.

3. Mr. Burton, (who / whom) is Anthony's father, met (they / them).

PRACTICE THE RULES

4. Sonya plays the piano better than (he / him).

5. He realized the job was done, and he'd done it all by (hisself / himself).

6. Give the package to Jim and (I / me), and we'll deliver it.

7. (Whose / Who's) car is (this / these)?

8. The decision was made by them and (we / us).

9. The store gave awards to two clerks, Sonya and (she / her).

10. The boat was purchased by Carl and (they / them).

11. He took George and (I / me) to the police.

12. (Whom / Who) is at the door?

Answers:

1. his or her	2. they	3. who, them
4. he	5. himself	6. me
7. whose, this	8. us	9. her
10. them	11. me	12. who

CHECK YOUR ANSWERS

1. In the sentences below, fill in the blank with the correct form of the pronoun that might substitute for the word or words under the blank.

Example:

I think Frank and __he__ are the best players.
          [George]

A. If you want something accomplished,

tell your problems to _____.
                    [Charles]

PRACTICE THE RULES

84   AFTER YOU WATCH THE PROGRAM

Subject Matter Review (continued)

B. From _____ do you expect to get the
[what person]
the money?

C. Nancy wasn't surprised that the winner of

the prize was _____.
[Nancy]

D. "To _____ is the package to be
[what person]
delivered?" _____ asked.
[Charles]

E. Bill's father and _____ often went
[Bill]
went fishing together.

F. The legislators should realize that it

is _____ who are at fault.
[the legislators]

G. We expect _____ and _____ to
[Ruth]   [William]
be here by nine o'clock.

H. The bills were late getting to
_____,
[Harry and me]
who are the bookkeepers.

I. _____, who are engineers, can't be
[Joe and I]
bothered with turning bills in on time.

J. Linda and Bill asked that the package

be sent to _____.
[their parents]

Subject Matter Review (continued)

2. "Ambiguous" means indistinct or confusing. Arthur read an ambiguous passage in the program. Here are some others that are ambiguous because pronouns are used carelessly. Rewrite each sentence to make it clear.

A. I'll hold the stake and, when I shake my head, hit it.

_____

_____

_____

B. She put the potatoes in the oven, the children to bed, and cooked them.

_____

_____

_____

C. The colonel chose Sergeant Smith for the assignment because he knew military strategy very well.

_____

_____

_____

_____

_____

D. The leaves were dry and I stood under the trees as they began to fall.

_____

_____

_____

_____

_____

Answers:

1A. him	1B. whom	1C. herself
1D. whom, he	1E. he	1F. themselves
1G. her, him	1H. us	1I. we
1J. them		

(Answers to question 2 will vary.)

CHECK YOUR ANSWERS

Quiz for Program 5

1. Circle the correct form of the pronoun.

A. The cab driver gave (I / me) and (he / him) a map of the city.

B. To (who / whom) should I return this check?

C. It was (they / them) after all.

D. The committee made (their / its) report.

E. This group finished before (they / them).

F. Gloria, (who / whom) is the librarian, furnished the bibliography.

G. Give (we / us) workers a chance, and we'll show you what production is.

H. The children admired the snowman they had built by (themselves / theirselves).

I. (He / Him) gave (they / them) bazaar tickets at a reduced price.

J. It is (I / me) (who / whom) was given a car just like (theirs / there's).

2. Fill out the chart below, choosing the singular or the plural verb forms to agree with the subjects listed.

Example:

everyone

is/are	was/were	has/have	doesn't/don't
<u>is</u>	<u>was</u>	<u>has</u>	<u>doesn't</u>

A. either of the cars

is/are	was/were	has/have	doesn't/don't
_____	_____	_____	_____

B. this kind of shoe

is/are	was/were	has/have	doesn't/don't
_____	_____	_____	_____

C. most of the profit

is/are	was/were	has/have	doesn't/don't
_____	_____	_____	_____

D. half the people

is/are	was/were	has/have	doesn't/don't
_____	_____	_____	_____

E. the book shelves

is/are	was/were	has/have	doesn't/don't
_____	_____	_____	_____

F. many of the trees

is/are	was/were	has/have	doesn't/don't
_____	_____	_____	_____

G. a sheep or goat

is/are	was/were	has/have	doesn't/don't
_____	_____	_____	_____

H. one of the fish

is/are	was/were	has/have	doesn't/don't
_____	_____	_____	_____

Quiz for Program 5 (continued)

3. Fill in the words missing from the chart below.

(today)	(yesterday)	(yesterday with helper)
A. I see	I saw	I _____ _____
B. I break	I _____	I _____ _____
C. I fall	I _____	I _____ _____
D. I _____	I began	I _____ _____
E. I _____	I _____	I have won
F. I fly	I _____	I _____ _____
G. I sing	I _____	I _____ _____
H. I talk	I _____	I _____ _____
I. I catch	I _____	I _____ _____

4. Mark the number of the error in this sentence.

<u>Pigeons</u> <u>is</u> a real health problem in <u>cities</u>   4.① ② ③ ④ ⑤
  ❶   ❷   ❸

where there <u>are</u> a lot of vacant buildings.
            ❹

<u>no error</u>
     ❺

5. Identify the spelling error.

A. 1) ninety   5A.① ② ③ ④ ⑤
      2) benifit
      3) grammar
      4) decision
      5) no error

B. 1) humor   5B.① ② ③ ④ ⑤
      2) lose
      3) athletic
      4) friend
      5) no error

Quiz for Program 5 (continued)

C. 1) noticeing
    2) receive
    3) studying
    4) truly
    5) no error

5C. ① ② ③ ④ ⑤

D. 1) secretary
    2) similar
    3) usualy
    4) quiet
    5) no error

5D. ① ② ③ ④ ⑤

CHECK YOUR ANSWERS

Answers for Quiz:

1A. me, him	1B. whom	1C. they
1D. its	1E. they	1F. who
1G. us	1H. themselves	1I. he, them
1J. I, who, theirs		

2A. is	was	has	doesn't
2B. is	was	has	doesn't
2C. is	was	has	doesn't
2D. are	were	have	don't
2E. are	were	have	don't
2F. are	were	have	don't
2G. is	was	has	doesn't
2H. is	was	has	doesn't
3A. I see	I saw	I have seen	
3B. I break	I broke	I have broken	
3C. I fall	I fell	I have fallen	
3D. I begin	I began	I have begun	
3E. I win	I won	I have won	
3F. I fly	I flew	I have flown	
3G. I sing	I sang	I have sung	
3H. I talk	I talked	I have talked	
3I. I catch	I caught	I have caught	

4. 2   5A. 2   5B. 5   5C. 1   5D. 3

Spelling Maintenance and Tips

SPELLING DEMONS

Remember when you were a kid and you spelled Mississippi like this:
   "M-I-crooked letter-crooked letter-I-crooked letter-crooked letter-I-humpback-humpback-I"?

As goofy as this sounds to you now, the technique involved here can help you with those words you just have to memorize. The fancy name for this technique is mnemonic (nee-MAHN-ick).

Memory experts use mnemonics all the time. Sometimes mnemonics are called "links," sometimes "bonds," but whatever they're called, mnemonics connect unrelated and ridiculous pictures to something you want to remember.

Ridiculous seems to be the guiding word. The crazier you can make the bond, the better chance you have of remembering it. For example, think of the word eucrasy. (This is probably the first time you've ever thought about that word, and that's why we chose it.) There's a way to remember the meaning, how to pronounce it, and how to spell it with one silly saying. The word means "to be in good health." So remember it by remembering this conversation:

Bill: "He's in good health."

Sue: "He? Eucrasy." (hE? U-CRASY)

Got it? With a little practice, you'll be able to make up silly sayings about words so you will be able to spell them.

Demons List

The Demons List this time is made up of words that most people just have to memorize. If you can use the usual method of remembering them, fine. If, however, you have difficulty, try making up some saying about each one and remember: The crazier the better.

A. debtor	F. thoroughly	K. lacquer
B. ensemble	G. vacuum	L. license
C. exhilarate	H. guaranteeing	M. lien
D. receipt	I. indictment	N. whereas
E. susceptible	J. irrelevant	O. dilemma

Special Demon

You can use the bond technique to tell the difference between words that sound alike but are spelled differently.

principle means a rule

principal means the principal of the school is a pal

Make your own bonds for these sound-alikes:

consul (a foreign representative)

council (an assembly of people)

counsel (advice)

Your Own List

Find some of your own confusing "sound-alikes."

_____   _____
_____   _____
_____   _____
_____   _____
_____   _____

When You Write

It's time for you to write something new. This time write three paragraphs only, telling someone how to do something. It may be difficult to find something to write about in such a short theme. Choose your words carefully, especially the pronouns you use. Remember all those things about grammar and usage that have been covered so far in this series. We'll work on this theme more in the next chapter.

Chapter
Six
Modifiers

In this program, Sonya and Freddy are preparing for a fund-raising variety show at Lacy's Department Store. They have to use Arthur's piano to practice, and Arthur has to suffer through many sessions of listening to Freddy trying to find an elusive C-sharp.

Their conversations are filled with descriptive words. Using these modifying words correctly proves to be a problem.

Sonya finally gets it right, though, when she writes an answer to a critic's unfavorable review of her performance in the variety show.

Watch the program carefully. The information it contains can greatly improve your writing skills.

Goal-Setting Exercise for Program 6

Complete these exercises and follow the Viewing Prescription.

Circle the correct forms of the modifiers in these sentences.

1. The student prepared his lesson (well / good).

2. It tastes (good / well) to me.

3. I don't feel (good / well).

4. Murray did a (real / very) nice painting job on the house.

5. Come out of your corners fighting, and may the (best / better) man win.

6. This beer has (less / fewer) calories than that one.

Answers:

1. well	2. good	3. well
4. very	5. better	6. fewer

CHECK YOUR ANSWERS

Viewing Prescription for Program 6

Check your answers, and then find the prescription that fits your situation by placing a check next to each statement that applies.

❏ If you got them **all right** …

we're proud of you! Enjoy the program, but listen for ideas that will help you with the workbook exercises.

❏ If you missed number **1, 2,** or **3** …

Arthur and Sonya give several examples of the correct way to use these tricky words. Practice examples are in the workbook.

❏ If you missed number **4** …

what does the program say about the proper use of *"real"* and *"very"*? Listen carefully.

❏ If you missed number **5** …

despite what they say in the boxing ring, the correct choice is "better" because this is a *comparison* between two people. The video should clear this up for you.

❏ If you missed number **6** …

for things that can be counted, use the word "fewer."

Vocabulary for Program 6

modifier (MAHD-uh-fie-uhr) is a word that changes the meaning of another word.

adjective (AAJ-ick-tiv) is a modifier of nouns and pronouns.

adverb (ADD-vurb) is a modifier of verbs, adjectives, other adverbs, and sometimes even whole sentences.

comparative (cum-PAIR-uh-tiv) is the form modifiers take to compare two things. For example: He is <u>taller</u> than I.

superlative (suh-PUHR-luh-tiv) is the form modifiers take to compare *more than two* things. For example: He is the <u>tallest</u> of the four of them.

LEARN THE WORDS

Subject Matter Review: Adverbs

Read the rules for the use of adjectives and adverbs, and complete the practice examples.

Adverbs modify action words.

Adverbs usually answer one of the following questions: Where? When? How? How much? How long? In the following example, <u>beautifully</u> modifies <u>plays</u>. It tells *how* she plays.

Sonya plays the piano beautifully.

LEARN THE RULES

Circle the proper forms of the words in parentheses.

1. Take out the trash (quick / quickly).

2. If you look (close / closely), you'll be able to see the mountains.

3. Sarah (definite / definitely) was finished with the work.

4. The whistle blew (loud / loudly) as the train entered the station.

5. The kitten climbed (clumsy / clumsily) out of the box.

PRACTICE THE RULES

Answers:

1. quickly
4. loudly
2. closely
5. clumsily
3. definitely

CHECK YOUR ANSWERS

Adverbs modify adjectives.

Example:

Harry is an <u>extremely</u> bright person.

The adverb <u>extremely</u> modifies the adjective <u>bright</u>. It tells *how* bright Harry is.

LEARN THE RULES

Subject Matter Review: Adverbs (continued)

Circle the correct forms of the words in parentheses.

1. It was a (real / really) successful day.

2. Doris had a (terrible / terribly) difficult job.

3. That is (sure / surely) a big house.

4. She heard the (disgusting / disgustingly) inaccurate story.

5. They walked onward into the (ominous / ominously) dark forest.

PRACTICE THE RULES

Answers:

1. really
4. disgustingly

2. terribly
5. ominously

3. surely

CHECK YOUR ANSWERS

Adverbs modify other adverbs.

Example:

The river flowed <u>very</u> swiftly.

The adverb <u>very</u> modifies the adverb <u>swiftly</u>. (The adverb <u>swiftly</u> modifies the verb <u>flowed</u>.)

LEARN THE RULES

Circle the correct forms of the words in parentheses.

1. This is the (more / most) (beautiful / beautifully) woven of the two tapestries.

2. Particles of dust are (extreme / extremely) (fine / finely) divided.

3. The situation became (real / very) (near / nearly) disastrous.

PRACTICE THE RULES

Subject Matter Review: Adverbs (continued)

4. Of all the animals, the apes (more / most) (near / nearly) resemble humans.

5. Canoeing in Alaska is my (more / most) (recent / recently) completed adventure.

Answers:

1. more beautifully
2. extremely finely
3. very nearly
4. most nearly
5. most recently

CHECK YOUR ANSWERS

Adjectives modify nouns or noun equivalents.

Adjectives usually answer these questions: What kind? Which one? How many? How much? For example, in the sentence below, <u>bright</u> modifies <u>person</u> and tells *what kind* of person she is.

Amanda is a <u>bright</u> person.

LEARN THE RULES

In each of the following sentences, an adjective has been underlined. Circle the word it modifies.

1. A snake was hiding in the <u>tall</u> grass.

2. <u>Expensive</u> cars were a passion with him.

3. He found <u>forty</u> dollars he didn't know he had.

4. The actress gave an <u>inspired</u> performance.

5. Did you see my <u>blue</u> bicycle?

PRACTICE THE RULES

Answers:

1. grass
2. cars
3. dollars
4. performance
5. bicycle

CHECK YOUR ANSWERS

Subject Matter Review: Adverbs (continued)

Use an adjective after a linking verb.

The play was <u>dull</u>. (It was a dull play.)

LEARN THE RULES

Circle the correct forms of the words in parentheses.

1. The plan seemed (sensible / sensibly).

2. They were (fearfully / fearful).

3. Negative reaction to the new regulation was (greatly / great).

4. The sunset was (beautiful / beautifully).

5. She felt (badly / bad) about the accident.

PRACTICE THE RULES

Answers:

1. sensible	2. fearful	3. great
4. beautiful	5. bad	

CHECK YOUR ANSWERS

bad/badly

<u>Bad</u> is an adjective; <u>badly</u> is an adverb. Use <u>bad</u> after a linking verb. Be sure to watch for verbs that can act either as linking or action verbs.

This is a <u>bad</u> day.
   (linking verb)
The pie tastes <u>bad</u>.
   (linking verb)
He tastes <u>badly</u>.
   (action verb—His tongue doesn't work?)
She felt <u>bad</u> about the accident.
   (linking verb)

LEARN THE RULES

Subject Matter Review: Adverbs (continued)

good/well

<u>Good</u> is an adjective; <u>well</u> can be either an adjective or an adverb. When <u>well</u> is an adjective, it means "satisfactory" or "in good health." Proper use of <u>good</u> and <u>well</u> is particularly troublesome.

They had a <u>good</u> time.
    (adjective <u>good</u> modifies noun <u>time</u>)
He played the game <u>well</u>.
    (adverb <u>well</u> modifies verb <u>played</u>)
I don't feel <u>well</u>.
    (adjective <u>well</u> means "in good health")

Circle the correct forms in the parentheses.

1. He hasn't looked (good / well) since his operation.

2. The car was (bad / badly) damaged.

3. The job was so (bad / badly); it couldn't have been (worse / worst).

4. Cynthia looks (good / well) in her Carmen costume.

5. Try to be prepared (good / well).

PRACTICE THE RULES

Answers:

1. well	2. badly	3. bad, worse
4. good	5. well	

CHECK YOUR ANSWERS

When discussing two things, use the comparative form.

Alice is the <u>smarter</u> of the two.
Alice is the <u>more</u> intelligent of the two.

Don't use comparatives together.

INCORRECT: She is <u>more better</u> than anyone else.
CORRECT: She is <u>better</u> than anyone else.

LEARN THE RULES

Subject Matter Review: Adverbs (continued)

When discussing more than two things, use the superlative form.

Max is the <u>tallest</u> of the four players.
This is the <u>most</u> expensive dress on the rack.

NOTE: Many comparative forms end in <u>-er</u>. Many superlatives end in <u>-est</u>.

shorter	shortest
older	oldest
smarter	smartest

Some adjectives and adverbs form irregular comparatives and superlatives. Here are a few of them.

	Comparative	**Superlative**
bad	worse	worst
good	better	best
well	better	best
many	more	most
much	more	most

Circle the correct forms in parentheses.

PRACTICE THE RULES

1. It was one of his (best / better) days.

2. She couldn't decide whether the red dress or the blue one was the (beautifulest / more beautiful / most beautiful).

3. The Tetons are among the (taller / tallest) mountains in our country.

4. He bought the (more / most) expensive camera in the store.

5. He is the (richer / richest) rancher in Texas.

Answers:

1. Either <u>best</u> or <u>better</u> works here.   2. more beautiful
3. tallest   4. most
5. richest

CHECK YOUR ANSWERS

Subject Matter Review: Adverbs (continued)

Avoid double negatives. Two words that mean "no" should not be used together.

INCORRECT:	I did<u>n't</u> spend <u>no</u> money at the store.
CORRECT:	I didn't spend <u>any</u> money at the store.
INCORRECT:	I do<u>n't</u> have <u>hardly</u> any money.
CORRECT:	I have <u>hardly</u> any money.

LEARN THE RULES

Circle the correct forms in the parentheses.

1. Don't give me (no / any) argument!

2. Neither Bill nor (any / none) of the others helped.

3. It wasn't (nobody / anybody) you would know.

4. Hardly (no one / anyone) plays croquet anymore.

5. He (has / hasn't) no business here.

PRACTICE THE RULES

Answers:

1. any	2. any	3. anybody
4. anyone	5. has	

CHECK YOUR ANSWERS

Skill Helper I

Adverbs fit into different places in sentences.

Example:

We packed the dishes <u>carefully</u>.
<u>Carefully</u>, we packed the dishes.

Subject Matter Review: Adverbs (continued)

Skill Helper II

Use <u>less</u> and <u>much</u> to mean an amount or uncountable quantity. Use <u>few</u>, <u>fewer</u>, or <u>many</u> to refer to things than can be counted.

Examples:

This dress costs <u>less</u> than that one.
This dress has <u>fewer</u> buttons than that one.

How <u>much</u> electricity does it take?
How <u>many</u> volts of electricity does it take?

NOTE: Beer commercials that say, "Our beer has less calories" are using incorrect form. Calories can be counted. It should be "fewer" calories.

1. Circle the correct modifiers in these sentences.

   A. Do you like tennis or handball (best / better)?

   B. Walk (slow / slowly) if you want to enjoy the trees.

   C. It was a (real / really) fine performance.

   D. There was scarcely (no / any) water in the tanks.

   E. Through (carefully / careful) observation, the scientists were able to solve the problem.

PRACTICE THE RULES

2. In the blanks provided, write the words the underlined words modify.

   A. Listen to the <u>delightful</u> song of the
       mockingbird.   _____

   B. It was <u>totally</u> unacceptable behavior.

                                             _____

   C. It was a <u>brisk</u>, cool evening.   _____

   D. Give the <u>crazy</u> thing back to him.

                                             _____

   E. Sarah was <u>terribly</u> afraid of spiders.

                                             _____

3. Fill in the blanks below with the correct comparative or superlative
   forms of the words shown at the beginnings of the sentences.

   Example: [short] This board is two inches <u>shorter</u> than that one.

   A. [good]   Of all the movies I've ever seen,

                 this one is the _____.

   B. [few]   There are _____ apples

                 this year than last.

   C. [strange] I may have heard a

                 _____ story, but I

                 can't remember one.

   D. [well]   Game four was the _____

                 one we played.

   E. [friendly] It might be possible to find

                 _____ spiders, but I

                 doubt it.

   F. [young]   We have three _____

                 kittens at our house.

Subject Matter Review: Adverbs (continued)

CHECK YOUR ANSWERS

Quiz for Program 6

1. In the blank below each underlined noun, write **C** if the noun is concrete or **A** if the noun is abstract.

> Imagine the <u>excitement</u> on that <u>day</u> in May
>   A) ___   B) ___
> of 1856 when 33 camels were unloaded at
>
> <u>Indianola, Texas</u>.
>   C) ___
>
> This first <u>arrival</u> was the <u>beginning</u> of
>   D) ___   E) ___
> the only Camel Corps ever commissioned by the
>
> U.S. Army. The <u>corps</u> operated with extraordinary
>   F) ___
> <u>efficiency</u> for the next nine <u>years</u>, delivering
>   G) ___   H) ___
> <u>supplies</u> throughout the Southwest, from Texas
>   I) ___
> to the <u>Pacific Ocean</u>. Its greatest <u>obstacle</u> was
>   J) ___   K) ___
> not the Indians nor the cruel climate but the
>
> <u>ridicule</u> it encountered everywhere it went.
>   L) ___

Quiz for Program 6 (continued)

2. Circle the correct word in each example below.

A. After the storm, debris was (laying / lying) all over the area.

B. Many people had (rode / ridden) out the tornado, huddled in makeshift shelters.

C. In one incident, a car was (thrown / throwed) 60 feet by the high wind.

D. Neither the National Weather Service nor the local weather station (are / is) infallible in predicting these storms.

E. The number of tornadoes in a year (is / are) carefully counted.

F. The boss asked (we / us) employees to stay after work.

G. I want the new job as much as (he / him).

H. (Who's / Whose) on first?

I. William and (he / him) got into the boat that belonged to (they / them).

3. Punctuate the following sentences.

A. Not this time said Phyllis

B. I am said William the most logical person for the job

C. When do you expect to arrive he asked

D. Bill said that he was leaving on the last plane

E. If you want to leave the oranges the apples and the rutabagas on the table

4. What corrections should be made in these sentences?

A. My Boss, Mr. Wilson, is in Chicago.   4A. ① ② ③ ④ ⑤
    1) remove the comma after <u>Wilson</u>
    2) change <u>Boss</u> to <u>boss</u>
    3) change <u>is</u> to <u>are</u>
    4) remove the comma after <u>Boss</u>
    5) no change necessary

B. Do you know who's bicycle sprocket this   4B. ① ② ③ ④ ⑤
    is?
    1) insert a comma after <u>know</u>
    2) change <u>sprocket</u> to <u>sprockit</u>
    3) change <u>who's</u> to <u>whose</u>
    4) change <u>this is</u> to <u>these are</u>
    5) no change necessary

C. There was scarcely no money left in the   4C. ① ② ③ ④ ⑤
    account.
    1) insert a comma after <u>money</u>
    2) change <u>scarcely</u> to <u>scarcly</u>
    3) change <u>was</u> to <u>wasn't</u>
    4) change <u>no</u> to <u>any</u>
    5) no change necessary

D. No one in the room left their seat.   4D. ① ② ③ ④ ⑤
    1) insert commas after <u>one</u> and <u>room</u>
    2) change <u>seat</u> to <u>seats</u>
    3) change <u>No one</u> to <u>Noone</u>
    4) change <u>their</u> to <u>his or her</u>
    5) no change necessary

E. He worked very carefully in the dangerous   4E. ① ② ③ ④ ⑤
    cavern.
    1) change <u>cavern</u> to <u>caveren</u>
    2) change <u>carefully</u> to <u>careful</u>
    3) insert a comma after <u>carefully</u>
    4) delete <u>very</u>
    5) no change necessary

Quiz for Program 6
(continued)

F. Theodore Roosevelt, who was President of   4F. ① ② ③ ④ ⑤
    the United States, was also an accom-
    plished athalete.
    1) change <u>President</u> to <u>president</u>
    2) insert a comma after <u>President</u>
    3) change <u>who</u> to <u>which</u>
    4) change <u>athalete</u> to <u>athlete</u>
    5) no change necessary

G. Neither the passengers nor the driver was   4G. ① ② ③ ④ ⑤
    seriously injured in the accident.
    1) insert a comma after <u>passengers</u>
    2) insert a comma after <u>injured</u>
    3) change <u>was</u> to <u>were</u>
    4) change <u>seriously</u> to <u>serious</u>
    5) no change necessary

H. Was the Alaskan canoe trip you're most   4H. ① ② ③ ④ ⑤
    recent adventure?
    1) change Alaskan canoe trip to Alaskan
        Canoe Trip
    2) change recent to recently
    3) change you're to your
    4) insert quotation marks ("") before
        Was and after adventure
    5) no change necessary

Answers for Quiz:
1A. A   1B. A   1C. C   1D. A   1E. A
1F. C   1G. A   1H. A   1I. C   1J. C
1K. C or A (Indians are concrete, but some obstacles might be abstract)
1L. A   2A. lying   2B. ridden
2C. thrown   2D. is   2E. is
2F. us   2G. he   2H. Who's
 2I. he, them
3A. "Not this time," said Phyllis.
3B. "I am," said William, "the most logical person for the job."
3C. "When do you expect to arrive?" he asked.
3D. Bill said that he was leaving on the last plane.
3E. If you want to, leave the oranges, the apples and the rutabagas on the table.
4A. 2   4B. 3   4C. 4   4D. 4   4E. 5
4F. 4   4G. 5   4H. 3

CHECK YOUR
ANSWERS

Below are five common words, but they have ten definitions. What each word means depends on how it is pronounced. Pronounce each word, then write a sentence using that definition.

SPELLING DEMONS

appropriate (uh-PROH-pree-ate) _____
_____
_____

appropriate (uh-PROH-pree-uht) _____
_____
_____

diffuse (duh-FUZE) _____
_____
_____

diffuse (duh-FYOUSS) _____
_____
_____

moderate (mod-uhr-ate) _____
_____
_____

moderate (mod-uhr-uht) _____
_____
_____

content (KON-tent) _____
_____
_____

content (cuhn-TENT) _____
_____
_____

produce (pruh-DOOSS) _____
_____
_____

produce (PROH-dooss) _____
_____
_____

Your Own List

Continue building your own list.

_____	_____
_____	_____
_____	_____
_____	_____
_____	_____

When You Write

In Chapter Five, you wrote a three-paragraph "how-to." Here is one for you to correct. It is filled with mistakes. Errors have been made in punctuation and spelling, as well as in the use of verbs, pronouns, adverbs and adjectives. First, mark each error. Then rewrite the passage so it's better.

```
You can make your own real beautiful station-
ery.

    Put some strips of paper and water in a kitchen
blender and grind it up.

    Repeat the above step until you have four or
five cupfuls of the gooey mixture pour it into a
cake pan that contain water. Stir the fibers slow
untill it is consistant.

    Dip the fibers on a screen even, turn the
screen over and place them face down on a newspa-
per. Sponge the screen so theirs scarcely no water
left in the paper. The screen lifts off. Press the
raw paper careful with a moderate hot iron.
```

_____
_____
_____
_____
_____
_____
_____
_____
_____

_____
_____
_____
_____
_____
_____
_____
_____
_____
_____
_____
_____
_____

Answer:

Here's one way to correct the errors:

You can make your own beautiful stationery.

Put some strips of paper and water in a kitchen blender and grind them up.

Repeat the above step until you have four or five cups of the gooey mixture. Pour it into a cake pan that contains water. Stir the fibers slowly until the mixture is consistent.

Dip the fibers onto a screen evenly. Turn the screen over and place it face down on a newspaper. Sponge the screen so there is scarcely any water left in the paper. The screen lifts off. Press the raw paper carefully with a moderately hot iron.

CHECK YOUR
ANSWERS

Chapter Seven
Sentences

Sonya nominated Mrs. Johnson for an award and is busily writing an acceptance speech for her. Sonya learns that putting things together in logical, clear sentences requires careful thought. She finds that one misplaced word can change a compliment into an insult.

Sonya sees that she must be careful not only of individual words but also of the way words affect one another when they are combined in a sentence.

Arthur talks about writing, revising, and rewriting. As an author, he is very familiar with this three-step plan for writing well.

Goal-Setting Exercise for Program 7

Circle the number beside the correct revision for each sentence.

1. The Brown family came to visit we like them very much.
   1) The Brown family came to visit, but we like them very much.
   2) The Brown family came to visit, and we like them very much.

2. The principal met with the students who drive cars in the gym.
   1) The principal met in the gym with the students who drive cars.
   2) The students who drive cars in the gym met with the principal.

3. All the wonders of Paris.
   1) All the wonders, of Paris.
   2) They saw all the wonders of Paris.

4. Phil spent Saturday mowing the yard, washed the car, and took a nap.
   1) Phil spent Saturday mowing the yard, washing the car, and taking a nap.
   2) Phil spent Saturday, mowed the yard, washed the car, took a nap.

5. If I would have changed the oil in the car regularly, I would not have ruined the engine.
   1) I wouldn't have ruined the engine in the car if I would have changed the oil regularly.
   2) If I had changed the oil in the car regularly, I would not have ruined the engine.

6. This shell is similar with the one on the beach.
   1) This shell is similar from the one on the beach.
   2) This shell is similar to the one on the beach.

Goal-Setting Exercise for Program 7
(continued)

CHECK YOUR ANSWERS
Answers:

1. 2	2. 1	3. 2
4. 1	5. 2	6. 2

CHECK YOUR
ANSWERS

Viewing Prescription for Program 6

Find the advice that applies to your situation by placing a check next to each statement that applies.

❑ If you got them **all right** …

SUPER! Enjoy the program, but look for those ideas that will help you make better sentences.

❑ If you missed number **1** …

this is a run-on sentence. Arthur has some tips for you.

❑ If you missed number **2** …

this is a sentence fragment. How can you take care of this problem?

❑ If you missed number **3** …

Be sure you understand what Sonya and Mrs. Johnson have to say about misplaced modifiers.

❑ If you missed number **4** …

Arthur talks about using the same form for words throughout a sentence.

❑ If you missed number **5** …

"Two <u>woulds</u> is one <u>would</u> too many," says Arthur. How does he tell you to correct this common mistake?

❑ If you missed number **6** …

Some usage is determined by tradition rather than rule. Be sure you study the list of such expressions in the workbook.

**Subject
Matter
Review**

The sentence subject should be clear to the reader.

Arthur said, "You want your subject easy to recognize." Study this chart, then answer the practice questions.

**LEARN THE
RULES**

Kinds of Subjects

pronoun	I, we, they	I should leave now.
noun	Sonya, rocks, talent	Some rocks are billions of years old.
noun phrase	the cow with white spots	The cow with white spots had a calf.
clause	who they are when they go	When they go is not important.
verbal	to know knowing	To know is to be.

In the following sentences, underline the subjects and circle the verbs.

1. Late that night, Arnold became lost on a country road.

2. Sleeping in a cool room invigorated the athlete.

3. Last spring, Susan and her brother, Bill, went to Europe.

4. Have you found your watch yet?

5. Those who are faithful will understand.

**PRACTICE
THE RULES**

Answers:
1. Arnold (became)
2. Sleeping in a cool room (invigorated)
3. Susan and her brother (went)
4. You (have found)
5. Those who are faithful (will understand)

CHECK YOUR ANSWERS

Run-on sentences confuse the reader.

Run-on sentences contain more than one thought. Arthur recommended four ways of dealing with run-on sentences:

A. Make two or more sentences.

B. Combine with a conjunction.

C. Use a semicolon.

D. Add a relative pronoun (such as that, which, who, whom, or whose).

LEARN THE RULES

Here is a run-on sentence, followed by examples of the four ways to fix it.

Friday we will have a ceremony, we hope all employees will attend.

A. Friday we will have a ceremony. We hope all employees will attend.

B. Friday we will have a ceremony, and we hope all employees will attend.

C. Friday we will have a ceremony; we hope all employees will attend.

D. Friday we will have a ceremony, which we hope all employees will attend.

1. Rewrite each of the following run-on sentences two different ways. Remember Arthur's suggestions.

   A. The large elm fell by the gate then the men came to remove it.

   _____
   _____
   _____
   _____

   B. The dog is barking it's keeping me awake.

   _____
   _____
   _____
   _____

PRACTICE THE RULES

Subject Matter Review (continued)

C. Give me some money I need to buy some gas.

_____

_____

_____

_____

D. Many young people want to be astronauts they dream of traveling through space.

_____

_____

_____

_____

E. Charles repaired the door, therefore, he was an hour late.

_____

_____

_____

_____

2. The following expressions may be correct sentences, run-on sentences, or sentence fragments. Write an **S** beside the correct sentences, an **R** beside the run-ons, and an **F** beside the fragments.

A. _____ Which belongs to my neighbor.

B. _____ Get the screwdriver for me.

C. _____ Even though it was the last one in the box.

D. _____ When in Chicago, Bill went to the Science and Industry Museum, he enjoyed it very much.

E. _____ Think of the world as a spinning top that is slowing down.

Subject Matter Review
(continued)

CHECK YOUR ANSWERS

Answers:

1A. … the gate. Then …
     … the gate, and then …
     … the gate; then …

1B. … barking. It's …
     … barking, and it's …
     … barking; it's …
     … barking, which is …

1C. … money. I need …
     … money because I need …
     … money; I need …
     … money, which I need …

1D. … astronauts. They …
     … astronauts, since they …
     … astronauts; they …

1E. … door. Therefore, he was …
     … door and, therefore, he was …
     … door; therefore, he was …

2A. F   2B. S   2C. F   2D. R   2E. S

Place modifiers near the words they modify.

Misplacing modifiers may produce sentences that are not only unclear, but also humorous.

LEARN THE RULES

Rewrite these sentences so the modifiers are in the right places.

1. The car belongs to the man with the racing stripe.

    _____
    _____
    _____

2. The newsman filmed the quarterback making a touchdown with a brand new camera.

    _____
    _____
    _____

3. All of the cars were not included in the Labor Day sale.

    _____
    _____
    _____

PRACTICE THE RULES

**Subject
Matter
Review**
(continued)

4. He had owned the house for 10 years which he
   inherited from his brother.

   _____

   _____

   _____

5. She could tell from his voice that he was
   sick on the phone.

   _____

   _____

   _____

Answers:
(Your answers may be different.)
1. The car with the racing stripe belongs to the man.
2. With a brand new camera, the newsman filmed the quarterback making a touchdown.
3. Not all of the cars were included in the Labor Day sale.
4. He had owned the house, which he inherited from his brother, for 10 years.
5. She could tell he was sick from his voice on the phone.

**CHECK YOUR
ANSWERS**

Use "parallel structure."

Sentences should use the same form of words throughout. This is called
"parallel structure." We have already discussed using the same form for multiple
verbs in a sentence.

Another troublesome construction problem is the use of <u>not only</u> and <u>but
also</u>. It is important to keep these constructions parallel.

For example:

NOT PARALLEL:

He not only lost the key but also the flashlight.

PARALLEL:

He lost not only the key but also the flashlight.

- or -

He not only lost the key but also lost the flashlight.

**LEARN THE
RULES**

PRACTICE THE RULES

1. The sentences below lack parallel structure. Rewrite them so they are correct.

   A. The carpenters will saw a hole in the wall, cutting glass and assembled the window.

_____

_____

_____

_____

   B. Afraid the bear would see him, Harold ran to the ridge and climb a tree.

_____

_____

_____

_____

   C. A waitress skillfully takes orders, delivering the food promptly and smiled, even in difficult times.

_____

_____

_____

_____

   D. Saturday was a busy day for Cynthia. She spent the morning doing laundry, washed the windows and clean the bathrooms.

_____

_____

_____

_____

_____

_____

   E. My job at the warehouse includes to make sure all the aisles are clear, stacking crates neatly and to drive a fork-lift.

_____

_____

_____

_____

_____

Subject Matter Review
(continued)

2. Rewrite these sentences using the not only / but also construction. Be careful that all parts of the sentence are parallel.

A. He not only visited the museum, but also the planetarium.

_____
_____
_____
_____

B. On his first day as a truck driver, Philip had a flat tire and lost his invoices.

_____
_____
_____
_____

C. Mr. Harris opened his mail not only to find his tax refund but also discovered that he had won the lottery.

_____
_____
_____
_____
_____
_____

D. When Sylvia drives through the countryside, she looks not only for old barns but also stops to pick flowers.

_____
_____
_____
_____
_____

E. Not only is Dick interested in collecting antiques but also fine art.

_____
_____
_____
_____

Subject Matter Review (continued)

Answers:
1A. will saw, will cut, will assemble
1B. climbed
1C. takes orders, delivers food, smiles
1D. doing laundry, washing windows, cleaning bathrooms
1E. making sure, stacking crates, driving a fork-lift
2A. ... not only the museum, but also the planetarium.
2B. ... not only had ... but also lost ...
2C. ... not only to find ... but also to discover ...
2D. ... not only looks ... but also stops ...
2E. ... not only antiques but also fine art.

CHECK YOUR ANSWERS

Use <u>would</u> correctly.

As Arthur said, "More than one <u>would</u> in a sentence is one <u>would</u> too many."
Although it may sometimes sound as though someone is saying "would of" (because we often slur the word "have" and pronounce it "uhv"), it is never correct to use the "would of" construction in writing. Do not write <u>would of</u>, <u>should of</u>, or <u>could of</u>.

LEARN THE RULES

In the sentences below, <u>would</u> has been used incorrectly. Rewrite the sentences correctly.

1. If you would have taken my advice, you wouldn't have lost your money.

   _____
   _____
   _____
   _____

PRACTICE THE RULES

2. You would of done better on the test if you would of studied more.

   _____
   _____
   _____
   _____

3. He would have felt better if he wouldn't have eaten so much watermelon.

   _____
   _____
   _____
   _____

Subject Matter Review (continued)

4. No one would have done a better job than he would have.

_____

_____

_____

_____

5. What would you have done if you would have been faced with the same situation?

_____

_____

_____

_____

Answers:
1. If you had … you wouldn't have …
2. You would have … if you had …
3. … would have felt … if he hadn't …
4. No one would have done a better job than he.
5. … would you have done, had you been faced …

CHECK YOUR
ANSWERS

Sentence Builder

In the next three chapters, we'll concentrate on giving you some insight into building better sentences. We'll apply all the things we've been discussing, so you can use them as tools.

Here's one way to build a sentence.

Step 1. START WITH A SIMPLE SENTENCE.
   The boy ran.
Step 2. ADD A PREPOSITIONAL PHRASE.
   to the store
Step 3. ADD MODIFIERS.
   tall   hardware
Step 4. ADD AN APPOSITIVE.
   named Bill
Step 5. ADD OTHER WORDS, PHRASES, OR CLAUSES.
   to get some nails

Put these parts together, and here's your newly built sentence:
   The tall boy named Bill ran to the hardware store to get some nails.

Paragraph Builder

A paragraph is a series of sentences that develop one main idea. As a rule, the main idea is expressed in one sentence, which is called a topic sentence. The other sentences in the paragraph support the main idea.

Read these two paragraphs. Identify the topic sentence in each one.

> **Home gardeners are a special breed of people. They spend the winter months poring over seed catalogues, believing everything they read. They walk their plots so early in the spring that they are in constant danger of frostbite. When they finally do get a crop, they invariably raise so much that they totally alienate their neighbors by forcing extra produce on them.**

> **We are so inundated with large numbers that we are immune to their meanings. A trillion-dollar deficit bothers no one. Hearing that there are four and one-half billion persons on the earth barely causes a raised eyebrow. Few people can grasp the size of a number if it exceeds 10,000, yet we hear much larger numbers all the time and ignore them.**

The topic sentence of each of these paragraphs is the first one. Topic sentences often are found at the beginnings of paragraphs.

Develop a paragraph using this topic sentence and details.

PRACTICE

Topic Sentence:
Searching for gold during the California gold rush was a perilous occupation.

Details:
1) Disease was common.
2) Violence erupted among the miners.
3) Starvation was a real threat. (Eggs sold for $50 a dozen.)

_____
_____
_____
_____
_____
_____
_____
_____
_____
_____
_____
_____
_____

Don't forget to keep looking for words you want to study and remember. List some of your "demons" below.

_____   _____

_____   _____

_____   _____

SPELLING DEMONS

When You Write

As we have mentioned, the main reason for improving your general knowledge of English is to improve your writing. To conclude this chapter, we want to introduce you to our FORMULA FOR BETTER WRITING. This writing plan is introduced in three sections, which we will practice and apply in the next three lessons.

Formula for Better Writing

Part I: FORM
          Sentences
          Paragraphs
      TECHNIQUE
          Correct spelling
          Correct capitalization
          Correct punctuation
          Imaginative word choice

Use this chart as a checklist for everything you write. Ask yourself if the sentences you write contain all the elements we have discussed. Have you removed all the errors we have warned you about? What about the paragraphs? Have you written a clear and concise topic sentence? Do the other sentences support the idea expressed in the topic sentence? What about your technique?

In the space below, write a three-paragraph "theme" about the room you are sitting in now. Try to follow the FORMULA FOR BETTER WRITING. We'll use this theme as a model to work with later.

_____

_____

_____

_____

_____

_____

_____

_____

_____

_____

_____

_____

_____

_____

Chapter
Eight
Organization

Order is the order of the day in this program. It's obvious that Arthur needs some assistance in organization, especially in his housekeeping.

Sonya helps him over some of the rough spots, but an argument with his publisher gets him into difficulty again. He wonders about not only the order of the material in his book, but also the relevance.

Will Arthur yield to his publisher's demands? Will Sonya be accepted for the supervisor training program at Lacy's Department Store? Tune in the program "Logic and Organization" for answers to these and other questions.

Goal-Setting Exercise for Program 8

Read the following topic sentences and the suggested details. Select the correct answer to each of the questions.

1. **Topic Sentence:**
    Police officers at the scene of Monday night's accident on Market Street were shocked by the sight of the jumbled wreckage.

    Details:
    a. The cars had been traveling at high speed.
    b. Sergeant Wilkins, a 20-year veteran of the force, said, "Those vehicles were totally unrecognizable. It's a miracle that anyone survived the impact."
    c. The driver of the westbound car was thrown 40 feet from the wreckage, but suffered only minor injuries.
    d. Not even the most experienced of the investigating officers could remember a worse accident.
    e. The driver of the police ambulance, Patrolman Hiatt, concurred with Sergeant Wilkins' statement by saying, "I see all of them [the accidents], and this one was by far the worst I've ever seen."

    Now answer these questions.

    A. Which of the following pairs of details should be left out of a paragraph with the above topic sentence?
        1) b and c
        2) a and e
        3) a and c
        4) d and e
        5) c and d

    1A. ① ② ③ ④ ⑤

    B. Which set of details below represents the most effective order for a paragraph with the above topic sentence?
        1) a, b, d
        2) d, b, e
        3) c, a, e
        4) e, a, b
        5) b, a, e

    1B. ① ② ③ ④ ⑤

Goal-
Setting
Exercise
for
Program 8
(continued)

C. Which of the following best states the   1C. ① ② ③ ④ ⑤
    "theme" for such a paragraph?
    1) a bad accident
    2) what Sergeant Wilkins thought
    3) the danger of high-speed travel on
        Market Street
    4) the way police officers viewed the
        accident
    5) one driver was hurled from the car

2. **Topic Sentence:**

    Marriage between sisters and brothers was a common practice among
    many of the original Polynesian peoples.

    Details:

    a. Only the female children from the brother-sister union were consid-
        ered "pure" enough to rule.
    b. Can you imagine the legal battles that such a practice would cause
        today?
    c. However, when the right mix of genes did get together, strong and
        beautiful children were produced, combining the best qualities of
        both parents.
    d. Such a practice accounts for the low moral level of the tribes.
    e. It was especially true in the matriarchal tribes that the queens were
        required by custom to marry their brothers.
    f. Missionaries labored for generations to show the natives the error of
        their ways.
    g. Of course, many of the offspring were genetically inferior, but since
        the culture practiced infanticide, the unfit were ceremoniously
        sacrificed.

    A. Which sentence most logically follows   2A. ① ② ③ ④ ⑤
        sentence G?
        1) c
        2) a
        3) b
        4) f
        5) e

    B. Which three sentences don't belong in   2B. ① ② ③ ④ ⑤
        this paragraph at all?
        1) a, g, f
        2) b, c, f
        3) a, c, e
        4) b, d, f
        5) c, e, g

Goal-Setting Exercise for Program 8 (continued)

C. Which of the following combination of sentences would make the most effective paragraph?

1) a, c, e, f
2) a, b, d, f
3) c, e, f, g
4) b, e, f, g
5) a, c, e, g

2C. ① ② ③ ④ ⑤

Answers for Goal-Setting Exercise:

1A. 3	1B. 2	1C. 4
2A. 1	2B. 4	2C. 5

CHECK YOUR ANSWERS

Viewing Prescription for Program 8

Follow the advice that fits your situation.

❏ If you got them **all right** …   you have what it takes to be a great writer! Ask yourself how this program was put together so it demonstrates logical development.

❏ If you missed number **1A** …   find out what Mrs. Johnson says about *irrelevance*.

❏ If you missed number **1B** …   What are the three things to consider about *sequence*?

❏ If you missed number **1C** …   How do our friends organize their ideas to best support the general theme of a paragraph?

❏ If you missed number **2A** …   What is said about *"transition words"*?

❏ If you missed number **2B** …   Be sure you study the workbook exercises on *"Fallacies."*

Viewing Prescription for Program 8 (continued)

☐ If you missed number **2C** …

You will need to pay particular attention to the video and the workbook exercises to learn more about *organization*.

Vocabulary for Program 8

LEARN THE WORDS

chronology (kron-AH-low-gee) refers to time. Paragraphs are often organized in order of time sequence.

unity (YOU-nuh-tee) means the way the ideas in a paragraph cling together. Thoughts must flow evenly from one to the next.

fallacy (FAL-uh-see) refers to misleading ideas. Fallacies in a paragraph destroy its logic.

irrelevance (ear-rell-uh-vance) refers to statements that don't apply to the general theme of a paragraph.

spatial (SPAY-shuhl) refers to space. This is one of the methods for determining the order of ideas in a paragraph.

inverted pyramid refers to a technique used by some writers, especially journalists, in which the main points are made at the very beginning of an article. Less important ideas and details are expressed farther along in the article. In newspaper writing, this is important because of space requirements. An article can be cut at the end without affecting the meaning of the story.

NOW WATCH PROGRAM 8

**Subject
Matter
Review**

Much was said in the program about topic sentences and the themes of paragraphs. Complete the following exercises. Your answers will be different from ours, but we'll give "possible answers."

Write topic sentences for the paragraphs below.

PRACTICE

1. They are built of exotic, extra-lightweight metals, streamlined to cut wind resistance as much as possible. Multiple speed transmissions, with 10, or even 15, gear ratios, are becoming standard equipment. Bicycles have become, by far, the most efficient means of transportation ever developed.

   _____
   _____
   _____
   _____
   _____
   _____

2. No longer are they at the mercy of network or cable schedules. They can watch what they want when they want. These emancipated viewers are even threatening advertisers because VCR owners seem to delight in pressing the "fast forward" button during commercial breaks.

   _____
   _____
   _____
   _____
   _____
   _____

3. Condors feed mainly on carrion, decaying flesh of dead animals. However, California law requires ranchers to dispose of dead animals immediately. Condors are suffering not only because of the law, but also because of people's repugnance toward decaying flesh.

_____

_____

_____

_____

_____

_____

4. Why should the raggle-taggle people in far-off lands wear my old clothes? What audacity lets me think that what's not good enough for me is good enough for them? If I truly wanted to help the unclothed of the earth, I'd send the missionaries my new clothes and wear the old stuff myself.

_____

_____

_____

_____

_____

_____

5. It seems that I'm the only one in the world who hasn't learned how to do it. No matter which way I move the hand mirror, it's always wrong. As a result, I had a bald spot the size of a dollar pizza before I knew my hair was even getting thin.

_____

_____

_____

_____

_____

_____

Subject
Matter
Review
(continued)

Answers:
(Answers will vary. These are just suggested responses.)

1. Even bicycles are going high-tech these days.
2. People who own home video recorders are developing a new sense of power.
3. The extinction of the California condor is assured unless both laws and attitudes change.
4. I don't give my old clothes to charity anymore.
5. I have never learned to see the back of my head in a mirror.

CHECK YOUR
ANSWERS

Transition Words

Arthur mentioned the importance of transition words, which lead the reader from one sentence to another or from the beginning of a sentence to the end. The flow must be even. Below is a list of such words.

LEARN THE
RULES

Some transition words and phrases show *spatial relationships*:

on the left
on the right
beside
above
further out
beyond that
behind
next to
in front

Some transition words and phrases show *chronological relationships*:

first
then
next
soon
while
after that
before
during
moments later
finally

Some transition words and phrases show *order of importance*:

first
even more
another
next
last
the most
least
less

Other transition words and phrases include:

Illustration	*Conclusion*
for instance	in summary
for example	thus
a case in point	consequently
Cause and Effect	*Comparison and Contrast*
therefore	on the contrary
since	although
as a result	similarly
	both

A sentence has been left out of the middle of the paragraphs below. Write a transitional sentence that does not break the paragraph's unity.

HINT: Read the first part of each of these examples. From the context of the first part, determine what must be said to lead logically into the next part. In the first one, think what it would be like to play chess with someone who spoke a language you didn't understand.

PRACTICE
THE RULES

1. Music is said to be the universal language, but it isn't; chess is.

   _____
   _____
   _____
   _____
   _____
   _____

   Your foreign-speaking opponent might not understand the term "checkmate," but he would certainly understand the condition.

2. Oh, how I yearned to have a pocket knife when I was a boy. To me, the name "Barlow" was the same as heaven. I fantasized about a pocket knife all day.

   _____
   _____
   _____
   _____
   _____
   _____

   When each morning arrived, the image of a bone-handled, tungsten-steel blade lingered until nightfall.

3. My Uncle George was a folk philosopher. He had a wise saying for every occasion.

_____

_____

_____

_____

"One boy's a boy. Two boys is a half a boy, and three boys ain't no boy at all."

4. You have to admire the department store metaphor of having the highest priced merchandise on the highest floors. The prices always work their way down from there to the bargain basement.

_____

_____

_____

_____

That is, unless the bottom floors are somewhere near the center of the earth.

5. Wild blackberries are overrated as far as taste and desirability are concerned. They are proof of the Thomas Paine saying, "'Tis dearness only that gives everything value."

_____

_____

_____

_____

The berries that half fill my tiny pail taste good only because I paid for them with hard work, mosquito bites, poison ivy and scratched arms.

Answers:
1. Even if you were playing with a Russian who spoke no English and you spoke no Russian, you could still play chess.
2. I dreamed every night for a month about the pleasures of owning a knife.
3. I still remember his favorite expression about the boys who worked for him.
4. The prices never seem to get low enough to match the condition of my pocketbook.
5. The blackberries I buy at the store for 40 cents a pint never seem to have much flavor.

CHECK YOUR ANSWERS

Subject Matter Review (continued)

Irrelevance

Paragraphs should support one theme or idea. You need to be careful not to say too much. Be certain that all the statements you make are necessary.

LEARN THE RULES

PRACTICE THE RULES

1. The paragraphs below have irrelevancies in them. Find them and cross them out.

   A. Harold took his scout troop to the State Fair. It was no small task keeping track of 30 energetic boys at the 102nd annual State Fair. Just getting them on the bus, which was owned by Bill Anthony, was a full day's work.

   B. Making stained glass windows is a painstaking art. Each odd-shaped piece of glass must fit precisely though not touch the next. It is an ancient craft. Space must be left to accommodate the cames, the lead channels which hold the glass in place. It is the soldering of the cames, however, which is the real proof of the art. The solder must have a high tin content.

2. Mark the number for the sentence that doesn't belong in each group of sentences listed below.

   A. 1) Writing a good paragraph isn't easy.
      2) The sentences should flow easily from one to the next.
      3) A good pen is a help.
      4) Sequence, the order in which sentences appear in a paragraph, makes a paragraph more meaningful.
      5) In addition, care must be taken to assure that all the sentences refer to one theme.

   2A. ① ② ③ ④ ⑤

B. 1) Talc is the softest and diamonds are the hardest.

2) Minerals of the earth are rated for hardness on a scale from 1 to 10.

3) All the others fall between these two extremes.

4) Chemical composition of minerals can be determined by burning them and observing the distinctive colors of the flame.

5) This knowledge aids rock hounds in identifying the minerals they find.

2B. ① ② ③ ④ ⑤

C. 1) They are able to handle ever greater volumes of information, and at the same time they cost less than they did just a few years ago.

2) Still, very few people understand the inner workings of a computer.

3) If automobiles had developed in the same pattern as computers, a Rolls-Royce would cost $500 and get 4,000 miles to the gallon.

4) They not only do more work and cost less but also are easier to operate than ever before.

5) Computers are getting more sophisticated and efficient all the time.

2C. ① ② ③ ④ ⑤

Answers:

1A. *cross out:* at the 102nd annual State Fair
     which was owned by Bill Anthony

1B. *cross out:* It is an ancient craft.
     The solder must have a high tin content.

2A. 3   2B. 4   2C. 2

CHECK YOUR
ANSWERS

Subject Matter Review (continued)

Fallacies

LEARN THE RULES

We've discussed many elements of a good paragraph. Now we need to talk about some dangers. It's tempting to try to support the topic sentence any way you can. Be careful. Fallacies can creep into your writing so that you will mislead your reader.

Below are some examples of fallacies that appear in writing.

Manufactured clothing isn't as good as it used to be. All the manufacturers are interested in is making a fast buck and keeping their unions happy.

The second sentence, which should be supporting the topic sentence, merely expresses the writer's opinion. Here is an improved version:

Manufactured clothing isn't as good as it used to be. A test conducted by an independent laboratory reported significant increases in what the researchers termed "shoddy workmanship" in the products of five major manufacturers. The same study showed a 30% decrease in durability of those products over the last ten years.

Here is an example of another common fallacy.

We have developed technology capable of sending people to the moon. Surely we can solve the problems of world famine.

This paragraph compares two things that are not related. These ideas can be compared, though, by talking about the problem-solving nature of both.

We have developed technology capable of sending people to the moon. That we have been able to do this should serve as a reminder that scientific problems are easier to solve than economic and political ones. If this were not true, we would have solved the problems of world famine long ago.

Here is one more illogical argument. Can you determine what's wrong with it?

The city is being ripped off by the construction company that's putting in the sewer. It would have been better to have put all that money into park improvement anyway.

PRACTICE

Subject Matter Review (continued)

Analyze these paragraphs and tell what's wrong with the logic.

Example: Jim keeps losing his key. He is either scatterbrained or just plain stupid.

Answer: There are lots of other possibilities. He could have a hole in his pocket. His keychain may be broken, or a thousand other things might be wrong.

1. Darrel, you are a great mechanic. You can fix anything on a car. Surely, then, you can analyze these paragraphs and make them better.

   _____

   _____

2. I saw on TV that a 15-year-old robbed a bank. The neighbor's son just got in trouble with the law. What's wrong with the younger generation?

   _____

   _____

3. Poor people wouldn't be so miserable if they'd fix up their homes and get better jobs.

   _____

   _____

4. He's guilty as sin. If he weren't, he'd have proved his innocence a long time ago.

   _____

   _____

5. Successful people look successful. All you have to do is look the part and success is assured.

   _____

   _____

Answers:

(Your answers may be different.)

1. Being a good mechanic is not equivalent to knowing about grammar.
2. Two examples are not enough for a sample. The generalization is too broad.
3. If poor people had better jobs (so they could fix their houses), they wouldn't be poor.
4. It's not his responsibility to prove innocence. He is innocent until proven guilty.
5. The conclusion is drawn from a statement that is unsupported.

CHECK YOUR ANSWERS

Quiz for Program 8

Complete these exercises.

1. Read the paragraph, then decide which of the numbered sentences best completes the paragraph.

A. Roger uses spoonerisms all the time. A spoonerism is a reversal of the initial sounds of two words, like "stew shring" for "shoe string." He claims it's accidental, "just the hay it wappens."
   1) Many people use spoonerisms.
   2) We've noticed, though, that he does it more often if people laugh.
   3) Some people think it's an illness.
   4) Spoonerisms get their name from Rev. William A. Spooner, who was dean of New College, Oxford, at the turn of the century.
   5) Roger's crazy.

1A. ① ② ③ ④ ⑤

B. More chickens are propagated in the world than any other domesticated animal. A look at their positive qualities will tell the reasons. They produce eggs, meat, feathers and fertilizer. More importantly, they produce jobs. The service industry connected with poultry is immense.
   1) No other animal, not sheep, not llamas, not even cows, is so popular.
   2) Chickens are very useful.
   3) The price of eggs is determined by many economic factors.
   4) Chicken feathers are not as important as they once were.
   5) Most popular breeds of chickens are hybrids which have been developed for specific purposes.

1B. ① ② ③ ④ ⑤

C.   A forest is more like a tapestry than a crazy quilt. Each tree is a community, including the bushes and small plants that live at its feet. Even the bacteria which change the fallen leaves into mulch are a part of the pattern.

1C. ① ② ③ ④ ⑤

1)   We don't really understand all of this.
2)   There must be a reason for it to be this way.
3)   This explains why the lumber industry replants the forests.
4)   It's as if there is a plan which allows nothing to happen totally by chance.
5)   Trees in a forest are very competitive.

D.   How far does a given spot on a tire travel during a thirty-mile trip? Obviously, it travels farther than the thirty miles because it doesn't move in a straight line. A specific point on a tire follows a pattern called a cycloid. Each time a 24-inch tire rotates once, the vehicle moves about 75 1/2 inches, but a spot on the tire has to travel 96 inches. That's about one-third farther than the straight-line distance.

1D. ① ② ③ ④ ⑤

1)   Therefore, a point on a tire goes farther than the car.
2)   So to go 30 miles in your car, a particular spot on the tire must travel about 38 miles.
3)   It doesn't really matter, though, if you reached your destination safely.
4)   The size of the tire makes no difference.
5)   This depends, of course, on how fast you travel.

**Quiz for
Program 8
(continued)**

2. In the exercise below, you need to do two things. First find the irrelevance, if there is one, and cross it out. Next, write a final sentence that "sums up" the theme of the paragraph.

A. Nature is very careful to assure that plants will survive. Notice how many seeds a maple tree produces. Can you imagine what would happen if every seed grew into a mature tree? The special winged seed of the maple is not unique in the world of plants.

_____
_____
_____
_____
_____
_____

B. Many people enjoy feeding birds in the winter. Commercial preparation of birdseed has become a growing business in the past few years. It is important that people who feed birds realize that they have taken on a long-term responsibility. Birds become conditioned to going to a certain place to feed. Once the feeding has begun, it is necessary to continue providing food for the birds.

_____
_____
_____
_____
_____
_____
_____
_____
_____
_____

Quiz for Program 8 (continued)

C. The price of shoes is a good economic indicator. For generations, a good pair of shoes has cost about the same as a day's wages. Great-grandfather could buy a pair of shoes for a dollar. Shoes cost a great deal more now than they did three generations ago even if they are made completely by machine. You may have to pay $50 for a pair of shoes, but this is no more difficult for you than it was for your ancestor to have paid a dollar.

_____

_____

_____

_____

_____

_____

Answers:

1A. 2　　1B. 1　　1C. 4　　1D. 2

2A. *cross out*—The special winged seed of the maple is not unique.
summary—Obviously, not all seeds can mature, but enough do to keep the species thriving.

2B. *cross out*—Commercial preparation of birdseed has become a growing business in the past few years.
summary—Otherwise, the birds might suffer as much or more than they would have had they not been "helped" at all.

2C. *cross out*—Shoes cost a great deal more now than they did three generations ago even if they are made completely by machine.
summary—Your daily income is in proportion to the daily income of your great-grandfather, so it all balances out.

CHECK YOUR ANSWERS

Here is another list of "Demons." Use the SEE-SAY-WRITE study plan to learn to spell them. Then, in the space provided, write a paragraph using as many of the words as possible. A dictionary is a good place to start if you don't know what a word means.

A. drastic　　　E. repugnant　　　I. amicable
B. odious　　　 F. temporary　　　J. tangible
C. copious　　　G. audible　　　　K. momentous
D. obligatory　 H. irrelevant

SPELLING DEMONS

_____

_____

_____

_____

_____

_____

When You Write

In chapter Seven we introduced the first part of our FORMULA FOR BETTER WRITING. Here is the second part.

Formula for Better Writing

Part II: ORGANIZATION
                Topic clear
                Sequence logical
                Ideas supported realistically
                Summation
            TECHNIQUE
                Correct subject and verb agreement
                Correct use of modifiers
                Correct use of clauses and phrases
                Imaginative word choice

This exercise has two parts. First go back to Chapter Seven and re-read the two paragraphs under the heading "Paragraph Builder." Study the topic sentences. You will notice that the topic sentence of the second paragraph isn't so easy to determine. In the space below, rewrite paragraph 2 so it has more unity.

_____

_____

_____

_____

_____

_____

_____

_____

_____

_____

_____

Now, rewrite the "theme" you wrote in Chapter Seven. This time, be especially careful to follow the suggestions made in this chapter. Follow the FORMULA FOR BETTER WRITING—PART TWO.

_____

_____

_____

_____

_____

_____

_____

_____

_____

_____

Chapter Nine Style

Clear, uncluttered and precise expression is what this program is all about.

Brenda, Mr. Edwards' secretary, and Sonya have trouble with sound-alike words. Meanwhile, Freddy learns that an insurance claim is intended to be a straightforward presentation of facts, not a flowery work of art filled with extravagant, high-sounding phrases.

Communicating what you mean in simple and direct language is a skill which must be practiced. Arthur suggests that omitting unnecessary words is a place to begin. He also tells how to make sentences more forceful.

This program is filled with important writing improvement suggestions. Don't get so wrapped up in the story that you miss the main ideas.

Remember this saying: "It's best to call a spade a spade. You can call a spade 'a durned old shovel' if you want to, but never call it 'an implement for excavation.'"

Goal-Setting Exercise for Program 9

Some sentences in column A are not clear; some are too wordy; others are weak for other reasons. Before each sentence in column A, write the letter of the sentence in column B that is weak for the same reason.

Column A

___ 1. Bill was on the lake fishing by 6:00 a.m. in the morning.

___ 2. The couple had a sumptuous repast at a local culinary establishment.

___ 3. The improvements were made by the Acme Construction Company.

___ 4. The children left dirty dishes on the table so Mary put them in the dishwasher.

___ 5. Farmers don't like wet spring weather because you can't make a profit if you can't get a crop in the ground.

___ 6. The continual flow of the river wore away the rocks.

___ 7. Harold lead the lost hunters back to their camp.

Column B

A. Suzie was proud of the antique weather vein she had just purchased.

B. During the course of the evening, the TV news reported that the ship was totally destroyed before it had reached its final destination.

C. Amanda tried not to detract the students from their work.

D. The vandalized statues were found by the police with holes in their heads.

E. The excited feline lashed out and lacerated the child's brow.

F. In "The Secret Life of Walter Mitty," by James Thurber, it tells about a hen-pecked husband.

G. The gate behind the garage was closed by Phil.

Goal-Setting Exercise for Program 9 (continued)

Answers for Goal-Setting Exercise:

1. B   2. E   3. G   4. D
5. F   6. C   7. A

CHECK YOUR ANSWERS

Viewing Prescription for Program 9

❏ If you got them **all right** …

You're marvelous, you know that? Enjoy the program. Be sure you complete the exercises in the workbook.

❏ If you missed number **1** …

Watch for the discussion of *redundancy*.

❏ If you missed number **2** …

Too flowery! Familiar, expressive words are much better than showy ones.

❏ If you missed number **3** …

Listen carefully to what Arthur and Mrs. Johnson say about *active and passive voice*.

❏ If you missed number **4** …

Be careful of *misplaced modifiers*.

❏ If you missed number **5** …

Arthur talks about the use of *indefinite pronouns*. Be sure you do the practice examples in the workbook.

❏ If you missed number **6** …

These sentences use incorrect words. Pay close attention to what is said in the video.

❏ If you missed number **7** …

The wrong words in these sentences are "homonyms." The past tense of lead (pronounced LEED) is led. When lead is pronounced LED, it refers to the metal. The device Suzie purchased is a "weather vane." A vein carries blood.

Vocabulary for Program 9

redundant (ree-DUN-duhnt) means saying the same thing more than once. It's unnecessary to say "a youthful child" because "child" means "youthful."

homonym (HAH-moh-nim) refers to words that sound the same but have different meanings. Example: <u>here</u> and <u>hear</u>.

ambiguous (am-BIG-you-us) means unclear and confusing. Ambiguous sentences result from poor word choice or arrangement.

indefinite pronouns The words <u>it</u>, <u>you</u> and <u>they</u> should not be used in formal writing unless they refer to definite antecedents.

LEARN THE WORDS

NOW WATCH PROGRAM 9

Subject Matter Review

Have you heard the story about the knife thrower who became so angry with his assistant that he decided to kill her? He reasoned that if he hit her with a knife, everyone would think it just was an unfortunate accident. Well, he tried, but he couldn't do it. He had practiced so long trying to miss her that he couldn't hit her.

This first review exercise is a lot like the knife thrower story. We've worked to get redundancies out of sentences. Now we want you to intentionally put them in.

All of the sentences below are redundant. Rewrite them so they are correct. Next comes the hard part. Write five sentences of your own that contain redundancies.

PRACTICE

1. He made a list of the requirements needed to
   totally complete the job.

   _____
   _____
   _____
   _____
   _____
   _____

2. He found a rope that was long in length and
   cheap in price.

   _____
   _____
   _____
   _____

3. The true facts of the matter are accurate
   enough, but in my opinion, I think they want
   us to descend down the road to destruction.

   _____
   _____
   _____
   _____
   _____
   _____

4. The store offered a free gift to all customers who were in the store at 7 p.m. in the evening.

_____

_____

_____

_____

5. Repeat again how you drove by car to the top of the ridge.

_____

_____

Now you're on your own.

6. _____

_____

_____

_____

_____

7. _____

_____

_____

_____

_____

8. _____

_____

_____

_____

_____

9. _____

_____

_____

_____

_____

Subject Matter Review (continued)

10. _____
    _____
    _____
    _____
    _____
    _____

Answers:
1. He made a list of the requirements to complete the job.
2. He found a rope that was long and cheap.
3. The facts are accurate, but in my opinion, they will lead us down the road to destruction.
4. The store offered a gift to all customers who were in the store at 7 p.m.
5. Repeat how you drove to the top of the ridge.

CHECK YOUR ANSWERS

Skill Helper

Remember the KISS formula. (Keep It Simple, Stupid)

Here is a list of common redundancies you should avoid. In each case, the underlined word is all you need.

LEARN THE RULES

actually <u>happened</u>

<u>accidents</u> that occur

advance <u>planning</u>

<u>adequate</u> enough

<u>autobiography</u> of his life

<u>before</u> in the past

<u>cheap</u> in price

combined <u>together</u>

<u>during</u> the course of

every <u>once in a while</u>

fatal <u>death</u>

<u>first</u> and foremost

<u>green</u> in color

hopeful <u>optimism</u>

huge <u>throng</u>

<u>if</u> and when

<u>inside</u> of

invited <u>guest</u>

<u>long</u> length of time

<u>modern homes</u> of today

<u>one</u> and only

one and the <u>same</u>

<u>rarely</u> ever

<u>round</u> in shape

<u>small</u> in size

the two <u>twins</u>

<u>throughout the</u> whole <u>night</u>

totally <u>destroyed</u>

true <u>facts</u>

Below are some sentences which are much too flowery. Rewrite them so they say the same thing but are more reasonable-sounding.

**PRACTICE
THE RULES**

1. It was my extreme good fortune to have had the opportunity to converse at length with an acquaintance of yesteryear.

   _____

   _____

   _____

   _____

2. May I call your attention to the splendid coloration of the last light of day?

   _____

   _____

   _____

   _____

3. We traversed the crowded thoroughfare, ardently seeking diversion only the cinema could provide.

   _____

   _____

   _____

   _____

4. When the nocturnal angleworms emerged, we captured a sizable cache to supply our piscatorial adventure.

   _____

   _____

   _____

   _____

5. As the ancient proverb expounds, "Prepare the cattle sustenance during the time of solar activity."

   _____

   _____

   _____

   _____

Subject Matter Review (continued)

Answers:

1. I was lucky to have had a long talk with an old friend.
2. Look at the beautiful sunset.
3. Looking for a good movie, we crossed the busy street.
4. When the nightcrawlers came out, we caught enough for our fishing trip.
5. As the old saying goes, "Make hay while the sun shines."

CHECK YOUR ANSWERS

Write sentences in active voice.

Active voice is more powerful than passive voice.

Examples:

The <u>hedge was trimmed</u> by Harold.

   (passive voice)

<u>Harold trimmed</u> the hedge.

   (active voice)

LEARN THE RULES

Change the sentences below so they are in the active voice.

1. Cookies were served by the Ladies' Auxiliary.

   _____

   _____

PRACTICE THE RULES

2. Mention was made of that problem by the engineer in charge of the project.

   _____

   _____

3. After the damage had already been done, the door was repaired by the carpenter.

   _____

   _____

4. The table was made by Roger, and the ceramic plates were made by his wife.

   _____

   _____

5. The beautiful flowerbed was planted by Kathy.

   _____

   _____

Subject Matter Review (continued)

Answers:

1. The Ladies' Auxiliary served cookies.
2. The engineer in charge of the project mentioned the problem.
3. The carpenter repaired the door after the damage was done.
4. Roger made the table, and his wife made the ceramic plates.
5. Kathy planted the beautiful flowerbed.

CHECK YOUR ANSWERS

Use a lively style.

Here are some suggestions that will help your writing come alive.

Suggestion 1:

Vary sentences by beginning them with adverbs.

He went along for the ride willingly.
Willingly, he went along for the ride.

Suggestion 2:

Vary sentences by beginning them with clauses or phrases.

She was an excellent mathematician although she was young.
Although she was young, she was an excellent mathematician. (adverb clause)

His favorite cup was on the top shelf.
On the top shelf was his favorite cup. (prepositional phrase)

Harry, running as fast as he could, jumped the picket fence.
Running as fast as he could, Harry jumped the picket fence. (participle phrase)

Suggestion 3:

Change phrases to objects.

Martha gave the theatre tickets to Roger.
Martha gave Roger the theatre tickets. (indirect object)

LEARN THE RULES

Each of the sentences below starts with the subject. For the sake of variety, rewrite them following the above suggestions.

1. Cynthia jogs two miles every morning before breakfast.

    _____

    _____

    _____

    _____

PRACTICE THE RULES

Subject Matter Review (continued)

2. The bookkeeper sent the check for the order to Ralph.

_____

_____

_____

_____

3. Harriet could see the beautiful sunrise from her window.

_____

_____

_____

_____

4. He learned to speak German studying by himself.

_____

_____

_____

_____

5. She looked at her old friend sadly.

_____

_____

_____

_____

Answers:
1. Every morning before breakfast, Cynthia jogs two miles.
2. The bookkeeper sent Ralph the check for the order.
3. From her window, Harriet could see the beautiful sunset.
4. Studying by himself, he learned to speak German.
5. Sadly, she looked at her old friend.

CHECK YOUR ANSWERS

Subject Matter Review (continued)

Avoid "stacking" modifiers.

Modifiers are nice, but don't overdo it.

Here is the example used in the video.

A battered, broken-down old airplane proceeded slowly down the bumpy, uneven runway and came to a shaky, sputtery, uncertain stop in front of a rotting, junky old hangar.

This is better:

An old airplane bumped down the crumbling runway and sputtered to a stop in front of a dilapidated hangar.

The secret is to find more expressive words to take the place of the many modifiers.

LEARN THE RULES

Rewrite these sentences. Replace the over-abundance of modifiers with words that say the same thing more clearly. (Answers will vary a great deal.)

1. The sparkling, dancing waters of the gushing little stream ran gleefully through the slimy, moss-covered rocks.

_____

_____

_____

_____

_____

_____

PRACTICE THE RULES

2. As they walked through the ominously quiet, dark forest, the chilling, awesome fear that they were lost sneaked into their weary, anxious minds.

_____

_____

_____

_____

_____

_____

_____

_____

_____

_____

_____

3. She stacked four lovely, delicious pancakes,
   smothered with melted, steaming butter,
   virtually swimming in luscious maple syrup,
   on his plate.

   _____
   _____
   _____
   _____
   _____
   _____

4. It was one of those wistfully lazy, hot
   summer days when no cooling, refreshing
   breeze stirred the stiflingly hot air.

   _____
   _____
   _____
   _____
   _____
   _____

5. After the swirling, beating snow had
   mercifully stopped, the noble, intrepid
   explorers, aided by their strong and faithful
   dog team, started again across the bleak and
   frozen tundra.

   _____
   _____
   _____
   _____
   _____
   _____
   _____
   _____
   _____
   _____
   _____

The sentences below suffer from those style problems discussed in this chapter. Rewrite them so they are better.

1. If a person works hard, you can succeed.

_____

_____

_____

_____

_____

_____

2. Give the window to the carpenter with the broken pane.

_____

_____

_____

_____

_____

_____

3. During Bill and Roger's argument, a chair was broken.

_____

_____

_____

_____

_____

_____

4. Would you be so kind as to direct me to the proprietor of this establishment?

_____

_____

_____

_____

_____

5. Every once in a while you find a situation that is equally as baffling as any and all you've encountered before in the past.

_____
_____
_____
_____
_____
_____

6. The tire was flat, and beside that we had left the jack at home.

_____
_____
_____
_____
_____
_____

7. The plumber found the trouble in the waist trap.

_____
_____
_____
_____
_____
_____

8. In the rules, it states that that's an error.

_____
_____
_____
_____
_____
_____

9. The UFO was round in shape. It flew in the air at a rapid rate of speed.

_____
_____
_____
_____
_____
_____

Quiz for Program 9
(continued)

10. The document was signed by all seven representatives.

_____

_____

_____

_____

_____

_____

Answers:

1. A person who works hard can succeed.
2. Give the window with the broken pane to the carpenter.
3. Bill and Roger broke a chair during their argument.
4. May I see the manager?
5. Occasionally you find a situation that is as baffling as any you've encountered before.
6. The tire was flat, and besides that we had left the jack at home.
7. The plumber found the trouble in the waste trap.
8. The rules state that's an error.
9. The UFO was round. It flew rapidly.
   (Better still: The round UFO flew rapidly.)
10. All seven representatives signed the document.

CHECK YOUR ANSWERS

Homonyms are pairs of words that sound alike but have different meanings and different spellings. Here is a list of troublesome "sound-alikes." Study their meanings and learn to spell them. This is just a representative list.

SPELLING DEMONS

accept = to receive
except (as a preposition) = but
except (as a verb) = to exclude

adverse = contrary, opposing
averse = reluctant

affect = influence
effect (noun) = result
effect (verb) = to bring about

allusion = indirect reference
illusion = misleading

avocation = hobby
vocation = career

beside = by the side of
besides = in addition

complement = to make complete
   or add to the meaning
compliment = praise

continual = repeated
continuous = uninterrupted

emigrant = one who leaves a
   country
immigrant = one who enters
   another country

loose = not tight
lose = misplace

perpetrate = to commit
perpetuate = to make lasting

principal = main one
principle = rule

respectfully = with respect given
respectively = in the order

Other homonyms to study:

ascent, assent	muscle, mussel
berry, bury	plain, plane
bridal, bridle	pore, pour
capital, capitol	profit, prophet
coarse, course	quarts, quartz
core, corps	rap, wrap
die, dye	read, reed
fair, fare	shear, sheer
foreword, forward	stationary, stationery
fort, forte	steal, steel
gild, guild	ode, owed
groan, grown	thyme, time
hail, hale	vain, vane, vein
hew, hue	yolk, yoke
it's, its	
main, mane	

When You Write

Now it's time to put together all those elements of writing that have been discussed throughout this series.

Formula for Better Writing

Part III: CONTENT
Is it accurate?
Is it expressive, clear, and concise?
Is it interesting?
TECHNIQUE
Follows the rules of grammar
Uses figurative language to advantage
Uses modifiers imaginatively
Omits unnecessary words
Supports arguments logically

Simply stated, good writing is direct and logical and moves smoothly from one idea to the next.

Here's one more tip before you write: Know where to begin and to stop. This sounds simple, but it isn't.

First, limit your topic. You can't write an essay called "American History" and do it justice unless you plan on writing a whole library full of books. The topic is too large.

Next, decide the way it will be organized. Will you use a chronological approach? Will you mention things in order of importance?

Finally, organize your thoughts before you start to write. Try to visualize the beginning; get your reader interested. Think about the middle; explain and support the theme with examples. Develop an ending that includes a logical summation of the whole theme.

Write a short theme about your hobby. Be certain you follow the suggestions in the FORMULA FOR BETTER WRITING. Use the information from the previous chapters to check your work.

Chapter
Ten
Review

**Preview
of the
Video**

Program Ten reviews the main points to remember from the entire series.

Notice how Sonya's use of the language has improved since the early programs.

NOW
WATCH
PROGRAM
10

Subject Matter Review: Part A

We want to review the subject matter in this program by using three types of questions. In this way, you can review the subject matter and also gain a lot of practice with each style of question.

Question Style One

To answer this type of question, choose the answer that is the *best*. Remember that whatever correction is made, *the meaning of the sentence must not be changed.*

1. We should of taken more care in our selection   1. ① ② ③ ④ ⑤
   of a building site.
   1) insert a comma after <u>care</u>
   2) replace <u>taken</u> with <u>took</u>
   3) change <u>building site</u> to <u>Building Site</u>
   4) replace <u>should of</u> with <u>should have</u>
   5) no change necessary

2. He come to the house for lunch yesterday.   2. ① ② ③ ④ ⑤
   1) insert a comma after <u>lunch</u>
   2) change <u>come</u> to <u>came</u>
   3) change <u>come</u> to <u>had came</u>
   4) change <u>lunch</u> to <u>Lunch</u>
   5) no change necessary

3. The burglars, who were caught in the act,   3. ① ② ③ ④ ⑤
   admitted their guilt.
   1) replace <u>who</u> with <u>whom</u>
   2) replace <u>their</u> with <u>they're</u>
   3) change <u>admited</u> to <u>admitted</u>
   4) insert a comma after <u>admited</u>
   5) replace <u>were</u> with <u>was</u>

4. John was at the filling station on Market   4. ① ② ③ ④ ⑤
    Street pumping 87 octane gas into the tank of
    his blue Plymouth van.
    1) insert <u>he always goes there</u> after <u>Market</u>
        <u>Street</u>
    2) replace <u>87 octane</u> with <u>no lead</u>
    3) insert <u>therefore</u> after <u>Street</u>
    4) replace <u>on</u> with <u>at</u>
    5) no change necessary

5. Bill works for the state department of   5. ① ② ③ ④ ⑤
    agriculture.
    1) insert a comma after <u>Bill</u>
    2) change <u>agriculture</u> to <u>agraculture</u>
    3) change <u>state department of agriculture</u> to
        <u>State Department of Agriculture</u>
    4) insert a semicolon after <u>the</u>
    5) no change necessary

6. If it is raining tomorrow, will Bill the man   6. ① ② ③ ④ ⑤
    down the street mow his lawn?
    1) insert a comma after <u>raining</u>
    2) remove comma after <u>tomorrow</u>
    3) replace <u>?</u> with <u>.</u>
    4) insert a comma after <u>street</u>
    5) insert commas after <u>Bill</u> and <u>street</u>

7. Julius spent the summer reading books and   7. ① ② ③ ④ ⑤
    climb mountains.
    1) insert a comma after <u>books</u>
    2) replace <u>spent</u> with <u>spend</u>
    3) change <u>summer</u> to <u>Summer</u>
    4) change <u>climb</u> to <u>climbing</u>
    5) no change necessary

8. Immediatly after the game, the players,   8. ① ② ③ ④ ⑤
    exhausted from the effort, went directly to
    their rooms.
    1) replace <u>directly</u> with <u>direct</u>
    2) replace <u>their</u> with <u>its</u>
    3) replace <u>players</u> with <u>player's</u>
    4) change <u>Immediatly</u> to <u>Immediately</u>
    5) no change necessary

9. Martha and him were the only ones home.   9. ① ② ③ ④ ⑤
   1) replace <u>were</u> with <u>was</u>
   2) replace <u>Martha</u> with <u>him</u> and <u>him</u> with
      <u>Martha</u>
   3) replace <u>him</u> with <u>he</u>
   4) insert a comma after <u>him</u>
   5) no change necessary

10. I feel quite good, thank you.   10. ① ② ③ ④ ⑤
   1) remove comma after <u>good</u>
   2) change <u>quite</u> to <u>very</u>
   3) change <u>good</u> to <u>well</u>
   4) change <u>quite</u> to <u>real</u>
   5) no change necessary

11. This has to be the most prettiest picture   11. ① ② ③ ④ ⑤
    I've ever seen.
   1) remove <u>most</u>
   2) replace <u>seen</u> with <u>saw</u>
   3) replace <u>This</u> with <u>That</u>
   4) insert a comma after <u>most</u>
   5) no change necessary

12. The Honor Society conducted their meeting   12. ① ② ③ ④ ⑤
    Sunday afternoon in the park.
   1) replace <u>their</u> with <u>its</u>
   2) replace <u>their</u> with <u>it's</u>
   3) insert a comma after <u>afternoon</u>
   4) replace <u>their</u> with <u>they're</u>
   5) no change necessary

13. Philip loves to fish he caught a 20-pound   13. ① ② ③ ④ ⑤
    muskie.
   1) insert a comma after <u>fish</u>
   2) insert a comma and <u>but</u> after <u>fish</u>
   3) insert a semicolon after <u>fish</u>
   4) replace <u>he</u> with <u>He</u>
   5) no change necessary

14. Is this house copied from yours?   14. ① ② ③ ④ ⑤
    1) replace <u>from</u> with <u>after</u>
    2) replace <u>from</u> with <u>by</u>
    3) change <u>copied</u> to <u>copyed</u>
    4) change <u>yours</u> to <u>you'res</u>
    5) no change necessary

15. My friend, Z. Walker Jennings, wrote a song   15. ① ② ③ ④ ⑤
    called Tiny for his folk opera, Four Poems
    for a Small Planet.
    1) insert quotation marks around <u>Tiny</u>
    2) insert quotation marks around <u>Four Poems
        for a Small Planet</u>
    3) underline <u>Four Poems for a Small Planet</u>
    4) underline <u>Tiny</u>
    5) underline <u>Four Poems for a Small Planet</u>
        and insert quotation marks around <u>Tiny</u>

Answers:
For this review chapter, we've listed the chapter (in parentheses, after each answer) from
which the information was drawn. If you miss a question, go back to the original chapter
to find out why.

1. 4 (2)	2. 2 (3)	3. 3 (1)
4. 5 (8)	5. 3 (2)	6. 5 (2)
7. 4 (4)	8. 4 (1)	9. 3 (5)
10. 3 (6)	11. 1 (6)	12. 1 (5)
13. 3 (7)	14. 1 (7)	15. 5 (2)

CHECK YOUR
ANSWERS

Question Style Two

In this style of question, you're asked to revise a sentence or group of sentences. A portion of the question is underlined and your response is made in reference to the underlined portion only. The first response is always exactly like the underlined portion. If you do not wish to make any revisions, mark response ①. *Be certain that the revision does not change the meaning or the intent of the original expression.*

1. Henry loved the drama series on the television. He went to great effort to see each <u>episode though the star had recently run afoul of the law</u>.
   1) episode though the star had recently run afoul of the law.
   2) episode because the star had recently run afoul of the law.
   3) episode.
   4) episode, though the star had recently run afoul of the law.
   5) episode, consequently the star had recently run afoul of the law.

   1.① ② ③ ④ ⑤

2. In <u>March Indianapolis, Indiana,</u> opened a new stadium.
   1) March Indianapolis, Indiana,
   2) March, Indianapolis, Indiana,
   3) march, Indianapolis Indiana,
   4) March Indianapolis, Indiana
   5) , March, Indianapolis, Indiana

   2.① ② ③ ④ ⑤

3. Many scholarly studies have tried to determine how Americans <u>spend their liesure time</u>.
   1) spend their liesure time.
   2) spend their liesure days.
   3) spend thier liesure time.
   4) spend, their liesure time.
   5) spend their leisure time.

   3.① ② ③ ④ ⑤

4. Arnold told us <u>to set in the last row</u>.   4.① ② ③ ④ ⑤
   1)   to set in the last row.
   2)   , "to set in the last row."
   3)   to set, in the last row.
   4)   to sit in the last row.
   5)   to sit, in the last row.

5. Either the hens <u>or the rooster was</u> on the   5.① ② ③ ④ ⑤
   porch.
   1)   or the rooster was
   2)   nor the rooster was
   3)   or the rooster were
   4)   and the rooster were
   5)   or the rooster are

6. We were honored to have two excellent <u>conduc-</u>   6.① ② ③ ④ ⑤
   <u>tors, Mr. Wallace and him.</u>
   1)   conductors, Mr. Wallace and him.
   2)   conductors; Mr. Wallace and him.
   3)   conductors, Mr. Wallace and he.
   4)   conductors, Mr. Wallace, and he.
   5)   conductors Mr. Wallace, and him.

7. Because of the careful planning, the project   7.① ② ③ ④ ⑤
   <u>turned out real good.</u>
   1)   turned out real good.
   2)   turned out really good.
   3)   turned out real well.
   4)   turned out really well.
   5)   turned out real, good.

8. If she had turned off the <u>toaster, the house</u>   8.① ② ③ ④ ⑤
   <u>wouldn't of</u> burned down.
   1)   toaster, the house wouldn't of
   2)   toaster, the house wouldn't have
   3)   toaster the house wouldn't have
   4)   toaster, the house wouldn't've
   5)   toaster, the house would have

9. Martha walked to <u>the store and looks for</u> a
new coat.
   1) the store and looks for
   2) the store and looks at
   3) the store and looked for
   4) the store, and looks for
   5) the store where she looks for

9. ① ② ③ ④ ⑤

10. Sharon <u>had laid in</u> the sun all afternoon.
    1) had laid in
    2) had lain in
    3) had lain, in
    4) have laid, in
    5) shouldn't of laid in

10. ① ② ③ ④ ⑤

11. The company of <u>soldiers were boarding</u> the
train.
    1) soldiers were boarding
    2) soldiers was boarding
    3) soldiers were boarded
    4) soldier's were boarding
    5) soldiers, were boarding

11. ① ② ③ ④ ⑤

12. He is the <u>one whom deserves the award</u>.
    1) one whom deserves the award
    2) one whom deserves the Award
    3) one who deserves the award
    4) one, who deserves, the award
    5) one who deserve the award

12. ① ② ③ ④ ⑤

13. It was <u>a nice baked cake</u>.
    1) a nice baked cake
    2) an nice baked cake
    3) a nicely bake cake
    4) a nice cake
    5) a nicely baked cake

13. ① ② ③ ④ ⑤

Subject Matter Review: Part B (continued)

14. "Hallelujah," shouted the wise <u>man, "One of my predictions came to pass!"</u>   14.① ② ③ ④ ⑤

    1) man, "One of my predictions came to pass!"
    2) man "One of my predictions came to pass!"
    3) man, "one of my predictions came to pass"!
    4) man, "one of my predictions came to pass!"
    5) man, "one of my Predictions came to pass!"

Answers:

1. 4 (8)	2. 2 (2)	3. 5 (1)
4. 4 (4)	5. 1 (4)	6. 1 (5)
7. 4 (6)	8. 2 (7)	9. 3 (7)
10. 2 (3)	11. 2 (4)	12. 3 (5)
13. 5 (6)	14. 4 (2)	

CHECK YOUR ANSWERS

Subject Matter Review: Part C

Question Style Three

The third style of question is used primarily for testing your skill in sentence structure and punctuation. You may be asked to combine two expressions and supply the proper punctuation. As with the others, the resulting revision must not change the meaning of the original expression.

1. Neither the passengers nor the driver was on the bus.   1.① ② ③ ④ ⑤

   If this sentence started
       Neither the driver nor the passengers …
   the next word should be

    1) was
    2) were
    3) wasn't
    4) weren't
    5) were;

Subject
Matter
Review:
Part C
(continued)

2. The committee gave an award to me. It also   2. ① ② ③ ④ ⑤
gave an award to Veronica.

The most effective combination of these
sentences would include which of the following
groups of words?

1)   an award to us
2)   an award to each of us
3)   awards to Veronica and I
4)   an award to I and she
5)   awards to ourselves

3. The economy experienced dramatic improvement   3. ① ② ③ ④ ⑤
but still fell short of projected levels.

If the sentence started
     The economy improved …
the next words would be

1)   dramatically but still
2)   dramatically, but still
3)   dramaticaly and still
4)   dramatically, and still
5)   , dramatically, but still

4. Because of the new arrangement, the orchestra   4. ① ② ③ ④ ⑤
performed well last night.

If the sentence started
     *The orchestra's performance last night
     was …*
the next word would be

1)   good
2)   well
3)   good,
4)   better
5)   best

5. The tickets to the theatre were given to   5. ① ② ③ ④ ⑤
Randy by Martha.

If this sentence started
    Martha ...
the next words would be

  1) gave Randy
  2) would have given
  3) give the tickets
  4) might have given
  5) would of given

6. The window blew out during the tremendous   6. ① ② ③ ④ ⑤
rainstorm. The water ruined the carpet.

If this sentence started
    The water ruined the carpet ...
the next word would be

  1) therefore
  2) but
  3) next
  4) yet
  5) because

7. Melissa, the boss' daughter, wanted to borrow   7. ① ② ③ ④ ⑤
my car. She wanted to visit a friend.

Which of the following is the most effective combination of these
two sentences?

  1) Melissa, the boss' daughter, wanted to
     borrow my car so she could visit a
     friend.
  2) Melissa, the boss' daughter. Wanted to
     borrow my car. To visit a friend.
  3) To go visit a friend. Melissa, the boss'
     daughter, wanted to borrow my car.
  4) Melissa wanted to borrow my car to visit
     a friend, the boss' daughter.
  5) The boss' daughter, Melissa, wanted to
     borrow my car. To go visit a friend.

8. Martha is terribly ill. Her temperature has   8. ① ② ③ ④ ⑤
   soared to 104 degrees. She'll either have to
   go to the doctor or die.

   This would be a better paragraph if the last
   sentence were

   1) She'll die if she doesn't see a doctor.
   2) She should see a doctor.
   3) She will see a doctor or she will die.
   4) She would have seen a doctor or she would
       have died.
   5) She will die or she will see a doctor.

9. The hunter shot an elephant in a green hat   9. ① ② ③ ④ ⑤
   from the truck.

   If this sentence began
       From the truck, the hunter …
   which of the following would follow?

   1) in a green hat shot an elephant.
   2) shot an elephant in a green hat.
   3) was shot by an elephant in a green hat.
   4) shot an elephant, in a green hat.
   5) shot, in a green hat, an elephant.

10. Bill went to the movies. Sarah went to the   10. ① ② ③ ④ ⑤
    movies, too.

    The most effective combination of these sentences
    would include which of the following groups of words?

    1) gone to the movies
    2) had went to the movies
    3) went to the movies
    4) goes to the movies
    5) have went to the movies

Subject Matter Review: Part C (continued)

11. Virginia has great facility with the English language. She is an editor.

11. ① ② ③ ④ ⑤

The most effective combination of these sentences would include which of the following groups of words?

1) Virginia, an editor, has
2) language, she
3) Virginia she
4) language, however she
5) language, though

12. The storm destroyed several bridges. Hundreds of acres of farmland were flooded.

12. ① ② ③ ④ ⑤

The most effective combination of these sentences would include which of the following?

1) The storm destroyed several bridges, but also
2) Not only did the storm destroy several bridges, hundreds
3) The storm not only destroyed several bridges, but also hundreds of acres of farmland were flooded.
4) Not only the storm destroyed several bridges, but also hundreds
5) The storm not only destroyed several bridges but also flooded hundreds of acres of farmland.

Answers:

1. 2 (4)	2. 2 (5)	3. 2 (6)
4. 1 (6)	5. 1 (9)	6. 5 (8)
7. 1 (7)	8. 2 (8)	9. 1 (7)
10. 3 (3)	11. 1 (9)	12. 5 (7)

CHECK YOUR ANSWERS

About Composition Testing

More and more tests include a composition section that asks for a sample of your writing.

Usually, these test compositions are scored by trained readers, who use a system called "holistic scoring." Holistic scoring is similar to the scoring system for Olympic gymnastics. Several readers quickly read a composition, get a general "feel" for how well it is written, and give it a score. The scores from all of the readers are averaged to arrive at a final score.

What Composition Scorers Look For

Scorers do not use a checklist of specific items. Rather, their judgments are based on guidelines. YOU HAVE THESE SAME GUIDELINES. The Formula for Better Writing used in Chapters Seven, Eight and Nine comes from the holistic approach to composition scoring.

Topics Included in Composition Testing

Usually, the topic suggestion is in two parts. There will be a statement of a situation. You will then be asked to respond to this statement in a particular way.

Example:

> The United States has an enormous ability to produce food. We have a great deal of productive farmland and an agricultural support network that is so productive there is often a surplus. Many people believe that the United States should use this great capability to reduce the famine of the world. Other people believe it would be unwise for the United States to use this resource in this way.
>
> What are your views on this controversy? Support your position with specific reasons, details and examples.

How To Prepare for a Composition Test

Write! Write! Write! Write about anything and everything. Check your compositions against the Formula for Better Writing.

Read! Read magazines! Read books! Read newspapers! Find several articles that interest you and check them against the Formula for Better Writing. Notice how authors do all the things you've learned about in this series.

Tips for Taking a Composition Test

ORGANIZE YOUR THOUGHTS.

As a rule, you won't have an opportunity to rewrite your composition during the testing period. You have to get it right the first time.

WRITE A "GOOD" TOPIC SENTENCE AND PLACE IT AT THE BEGINNING OF EACH PARAGRAPH.

In general writing, topic sentences can appear anywhere in a paragraph. For testing purposes, make the first sentence the topic sentence. Don't get cute! Make the topic straightforward.

SUPPORT TOPIC SENTENCES LOGICALLY

Compositions don't have to be scholarly. They just have to support what they say they support.

BE CAREFUL OF FORM

A simple oversight, such as not indenting a paragraph, can hurt your score. Take care of all the simple things, including spelling and punctuation.

RELAX

Go at the task of taking a composition test as if it were one more exercise. If you have done all the exercises in this workbook, doing just one more is no big deal.

GOOD LUCK!

Post-Test

DIRECTIONS: Below are some sentences in which errors may or may not have been made. The errors may be in spelling, capitalization, punctuation, word choice or sentence structure. Read the sentences and choose the answer that best corrects each sentence. No sentence contains more than one error. If there is no error, mark answer ⑤.

1. I should have went to the bigger of the two stores.
   1) change should have to should of
   2) change went to gone
   3) change bigger to biggest
   4) insert not after should
   5) no change necessary

   1.① ② ③ ④ ⑤

2. The neighbor's dog came over yesterday about 3:00 in the afternoon and lay in the yard until dark.
   1) change neighbor's to nieghbor's
   2) change came to come
   3) insert p.m. after 3:00
   4) change lay to laid
   5) no change necessary

   2.① ② ③ ④ ⑤

3. Don't move too quick or you're likely to   3. ① ② ③ ④ ⑤
   fall.
   1) change you're to your
   2) insert a comma after quick
   3) change too to to
   4) change quick to quickly
   5) no change necessary

4. It was an uncomfortable arrangement, but us   4. ① ② ③ ④ ⑤
   workers completed the job anyway.
   1) change arrangement to arrangment
   2) remove comma after arrangement
   3) change an to a
   4) change us to we
   5) no change necessary

5. When Martha the committee chairperson read   5. ① ② ③ ④ ⑤
   the proposal, everyone applauded.
   1) insert commas after Martha and chairper-
      son
   2) remove comma after proposal
   3) change applauded to aplauded
   4) change proposal to perposal
   5) no change necessary

6. Historicly, the river rises every spring.   6. ① ② ③ ④ ⑤
   1) change rises to raises
   2) change every to ever
   3) remove comma after Historicly
   4) change Historicly to Historically
   5) no change necessary

7. "There isn't nothing I wouldn't do," said   7. ① ② ③ ④ ⑤
   Harold, "to live like a millionaire."
   1) change millionaire to millionair
   2) change isn't to is'nt
   3) change do," to do",
   4) change nothing to anything
   5) no change necessary

8. He saw a robber drive away from the bank in a   8. ① ② ③ ④ ⑤
1982 Oldsmobile <u>wearing a mask</u>.
  1) omit underlined part
  2) insert underlined part after <u>bank</u>
  3) insert underlined part after <u>robber</u>
  4) insert underlined part after <u>away</u>
  5) no change necessary

9. Searchlights on the shore illuminated the   9. ① ② ③ ④ ⑤
sinking ship and guides the Coast Guard to
the rescue.
  1) change <u>guides</u> to <u>guided</u>
  2) change <u>illuminated</u> to <u>alluminated</u>
  3) change <u>Coast Guard</u> to <u>coast guard</u>
  4) insert comma after <u>ship</u>
  5) no change necessary

10. If you want to know who was here first, it   10. ① ② ③ ④ ⑤
was me.
  1) change <u>who</u> to <u>whom</u>
  2) remove comma after <u>first</u>
  3) insert comma after <u>know</u>
  4) change <u>me</u> to <u>I</u>
  5) no change necessary

11. She knew Roger, the head waiter, though they   11. ① ② ③ ④ ⑤
had never been formerly introduced.
  1) change <u>knew</u> to <u>knowed</u>
  2) remove commas after <u>Roger</u> and <u>waiter</u>
  3) change <u>formerly</u> to <u>formally</u>
  4) change <u>though</u> to <u>tho</u>
  5) no change necessary

12. Martha asked, "How long have you been a   12. ① ② ③ ④ ⑤
member of the Democratic Party"?
  1) change <u>Party"?</u> to <u>Party ?"</u>
  2) change <u>Party</u> to <u>party</u>
  3) change <u>asked, "</u> to <u>asked ",</u>
  4) change <u>Party"?</u> to <u>Party."</u>
  5) no change necessary

13. Each of the ideas from Bill and him has   13. ① ② ③ ④ ⑤
    strong points.
    1) insert commas after <u>from</u> and <u>him</u>
    2) change <u>has</u> to <u>have</u>
    3) change <u>him</u> to <u>he</u>
    4) change <u>Each</u> to <u>All</u>
    5) no change necessary

14. The committee run into difficulty trying to   14. ① ② ③ ④ ⑤
    solve the troublesome problem.
    1) change <u>run</u> to <u>ran</u>
    2) change <u>troublesome</u> to <u>troublsome</u>
    3) insert comma after <u>difficulty</u>
    4) insert comma after <u>trying</u>
    5) no change necessary

15. Not only the book shelves but also the cup-   15. ① ② ③ ④ ⑤
    board was full.
    1) insert comma after <u>shelves</u>
    2) insert <u>was</u> after <u>only</u>
    3) insert <u>were</u> after <u>only</u>
    4) change <u>was</u> to <u>were</u>
    5) no change necessary

16. The people who came in the car are William   16. ① ② ③ ④ ⑤
    and her.
    1) change <u>who</u> to <u>whom</u>
    2) change <u>are</u> to <u>is</u>
    3) insert commas after <u>people</u> and <u>car</u>
    4) change <u>her</u> to <u>she</u>
    5) no change necessary

17. Harold told her the disgusting, inaccurate   17. ① ② ③ ④ ⑤
    story.
    1) change <u>disgusting</u> to <u>disgustingly</u>
    2) remove comma after <u>disgusting</u>
    3) change <u>inaccurate</u> to <u>innaccurate</u>
    4) insert comma after <u>inaccurate</u>
    5) no change necessary

187

18. This is the more beautiful woven of the two   18.① ② ③ ④ ⑤
    tapestries.
    1) change tapestries to tapastries
    2) change more to most
    3) change beautiful to beautifully
    4) insert semicolon after woven
    5) no change necessary

19. Sally, who is sitting at the end of the   19.① ② ③ ④ ⑤
    table, is taller than anyone in the room.
    1) insert else after anyone
    2) change who to whom
    3) remove the words in the room
    4) remove commas after Sally and table
    5) no change necessary

20. He not only visited the museum but also the   20.① ② ③ ④ ⑤
    planetarium and the art museum.
    1) change planetarium to planatarium
    2) move visited to after He
    3) insert comma after museum
    4) change visited to is visiting
    5) no change necessary

Answers for Post-Test:
1. 2)	2. 5)	3. 4)	4. 4)	5. 1)
6. 4)	7. 4)	8. 3)	9. 1)	10. 4)
11. 3)	12. 1)	13. 5)	14. 1)	15. 5)
16. 4)	17. 5)	18. 3)	19. 1)	20. 2)

CHECK YOUR
ANSWERS

Prescription for Further Study

If you made errors in the Post-Test, use this chart to determine why you made them. Review the chapters suggested.

On question	if you answered	you were wrong because	you should review
1.	1)	you should never use "should of"	Chapters 3 & 4
	3)	when comparing two things, use "bigger"	Chapter 6
	4)	it would change the meaning	Chapter 10
	5)	2) is the right answer	Chapter 3 & 4
2.	1)	there is no misspelling	Chapter 1
	2)	"come" is the wrong word	Chapter 3
	3)	adding "p.m." makes the sentence redundant	Chapter 9
	4)	the past tense of "lie" is "lay"	Chapter 3
3.	1)	"your" means "belonging to you"	Chapter 5
	2)	it isn't needed	Chapter 2
	3)	"to" is the wrong word	Chapter 1 & 9
	5)	4) is correct	Chapter 6

Prescription for Further Study
(continued)

On question	if you answered	you were wrong because	you should review
4.	1)	there is no misspelled word	Chapter 1
	2)	the comma belongs	Chapter 2
	3)	"an" is right	Chapter 6
	5)	4) is correct	Chapter 5
5.	2)	the comma belongs	Chapter 2
	3)	there is no misspelled word	Chapter 1
	4)	there is no misspelled word	Chapter 1
	5)	1) is correct	Chapter 2
6.	1)	use comparative form	Chapter 6
	2)	use comparative form	Chapter 6
	3)	the comma belongs	Chapter 2
	5)	4) is correct	Chapter 3 & 4
7.	1)	there is no misspelled word	Chapter 1
	2)	"isn't" is correct	Chapter 1 & 2
	3)	comma goes inside the quotation marks	Chapter 2
	5)	4) is correct	Chapter 6

On question	if you answered	you were wrong because	you should review
8.	1)	it would change the meaning	Chapter 10
	2)	you don't mean the bank was wearing the mask	Chapter 7
	4)	the mask didn't come from the bank	Chapter 7
	5)	3) is correct	Chapter 7
9.	2)	there is no misspelled word	Chapter 1
	3)	"Coast Guard" is right	Chapter 2
	4)	no comma needed	Chapter 2
	5)	1) is correct	Chapter 7
10.	1)	this answers the question "Who was first?"	Chapter 5
	2)	commas separate the clause	Chapter 2
	3)	this is not an appositive	Chapter 2
	5)	4) is correct	Chapter 5

On question	if you answered	you were wrong because	you should review
11.	1)	there is no such word as "knowed"	Chapter 3
	2)	", head waiter," renames "Roger"	Chapter 2
	4)	"tho" is not used in formal writing	Chapter 9
	5)	3) is correct	Chapter 9
12.	2)	"Party" should be capitalized	Chapter 2
	3)	the comma is right	Chapter 2
	4)	this is a question	Chapter 2
	5)	1) is correct	Chapter 2
13.	1)	this is not an appositive	Chapter 2
	2)	"Each" is the subject	Chapter 4
	3)	must use "object" pronoun	Chapter 5
	4)	"All" would change the meaning	Chapter 10

Prescription for Further Study
(continued)

On question	if you answered	you were wrong because	you should review
14.	2)	there is no misspelled word	Chapter 1
	3)	no comma needed	Chapter 2
	4)	no comma needed	Chapter 2
	5)	1) is correct	Chapter 3 & 4
15.	1)	no comma needed	Chapter 2
	2)	it isn't needed	Chapter 4
	3)	"were" is wrong	Chapter 3 & 4
	4)	"were" is wrong	Chapter 3 & 4
16.	1)	"who" is right	Chapter 5
	2)	"are" is right	Chapter 4
	3)	it is not an appositive	Chapter 2
	5)	4) is correct	Chapter 5
17.	1)	"disgusting" is right	Chapter 6
	2)	comma should stay	Chapter 6
	3)	there is no misspelled word	Chapter 1
	4)	no comma is needed	Chapter 2

On question	if you answered	you were wrong because	you should review
18.	1)	there is no misspelled word	Chapter 1
	2)	use the comparative form	Chapter 6
	4)	no semicolon needed	Chapter 2
	5)	3) is correct	Chapter 6
19.	2)	"who" is correct	Chapter 5
	3)	this would change the meaning	Chapter 10
	4)	this is not an appositive	Chapter 2
	5)	1) is correct	Chapter 6
20.	1)	there is no misspelled word	Chapter 1
	3)	comma is not needed	Chapter 4
	4)	this would change the meaning	Chapter 10
	5)	2) is correct	Chapter 4

Credits

National Advisors

BILL BOX
Supervisor, Adult Education
State Department of Education
Jackson, Mississippi

LILA CAMBURN
Director, Community Services
Pascagoula Municipal Separate School
    District
Pascagoula, Mississippi

State Advisors

ANN GEORGIAN
Hattiesburg High School
Hattiesburg, Mississippi

DR. MARIA HARVEY
Jackson State University
Jackson, Mississippi

DR. LINDA JACKSON
Northwest Mississippi Junior College
Senatobia, Mississippi

AUDRY KEITH
Meridian Junior College
Meridian, Mississippi

PATSY LUSTY
Itawamba Junior College
Houlka, Mississippi

LINDA LIPE
Jackson, Mississippi

THELMA PEYTON
Bay Springs High School
Bay Springs, Mississippi

RACHEL SCURLOCK
Charleston, Mississippi

ROSE WANSLEY
Callaway High School
Jackson, Mississippi

The Players

TRABER BURNS
Arthur

SHARI SCHNEIDER
Sonya

RENATO POWELL
Mrs. Johnson

ROBERT WILLIAMS
Freddy

MAC McMILLAN
Mr. Edwards

MARGARET GRAHAM
Brenda

ED SHELNUT
Personnel Officer

Production Credits

F. LEE MORRIS
Executive Director

LAWRENCE HOLDEN
Director of Production

PETER ZAPLETAL
Producer

FRANCIS X. RULLAN
Co-Producer & Director

JOHN WEBB
Writer

CONNIE QUEEN
Instructional Developer

OBIE ATKINS
Original Music

KENT BOWLDS
CLARENCE HOOKER
Editors

SANDY McNEAL
Set Designer

STANLEY GRAHAM
Lighting Designer

ANNETTE SPURLOCK
Production Assistant

DENNIS CONNEL
DAVID LANG
Audio

MYRA MORRIS
Videotape

EDDY RAY WARREN
Audio

EDDIE BUNKLEY
Field Recording Unit

BOBBY ARNOLD
Set Decorator & Props

ROY DUNCAN
Production Manager

JO ANN PRITCHARD
Consultant to the Writer

WILLIAM BENDER
TONY CARPENTER
MARCOS DEL NERO
EARNEST SEALS
GLENROY SMITH
IRENE TURNER
Production Crew

GERTHANIA McGEE
Switcher

BOB BRACEY
JACQUELINE MACK
CMX Operators

KENT BOWLDS
DONALD HUMER
Field Camera

KATHERINE MOORE
Costumes & Makeup

MOSELL LANG
SAVAN WILSON
CHRIS McGUIRE
Project Development

PETER ZAPLETAL
Electronic Graphics

BOB GARNER
Technical Director

RONALD DIFFENDERFER
KATHY RECTOR
Video

WENDELL BRELAND
Technical Director

BECKY KYZAR
Videotape

CHARLES NARON
JIM RANAGER
Set Construction

IRENE TURNER
Lighting Assistant

DOROTHY SULLIVAN
Script Editor

BOBBY COLLUM
Supervisor of Instructional Television

Write Right was produced at Mississippi
    Educational Television

National Advisory Committee Members, 1984-1985

Bob Allen	Texas Education Agency
Douglas Bodwell	Corporation for Public Broadcasting
William Box	Mississippi Department of Education
Lila Camburn	Pascagoula (MS) School District
Dr. Robert Clausen	Oregon Department of Education
Jean Coleman	American Library Association
Sharon Darling	Kentucky Department of Education
Samuel Delaney	Fayette Co. (KY) Board of Education
Paul Delker	U.S. Department of Education
Luke Easter	Tennessee Department of Education
Dr. Robert Emmitt	U.S. Department of Labor
Dr. Gary Eyre	Council on Education
George Eyster	Morehead State University
Joan Flanery	Ashland (KY) Adult Ed. Learning Center
Dr. James Fouche	Kentucky Department of Education
Virginia Fox	Southern Educational Communications Association
Alan Garinger	Author
Chuck Guthrie	Murray State University
Tom Hale	Jefferson County (KY) Public Schools
Dr. John Hartwig	Iowa Department of Public Instruction
Beverly Herrlinger	Louisville (KY) Adult Ed. Learning Center
Lawrence Holden	Mississippi Educational Television
Paris Hopkins	Kentucky Office of Vocational Rehabilitation
Nancy Husk	Louisville (KY) Adult Ed. Learning Center
Sharon Jackson	Morehead State University
John Keenan	University of Maryland
Gentry LaRue	Fayette Co. (KY) Public Schools
Christie Maloney	University of Louisville
Charlotte Martin	Wisconsin Board of Voc-Tech-Ad Education
Sylvia McCollum	Federal Bureau of Prisons
Garrett Murphy	New York State Education Department
James Nelson	Kentucky Department of Libraries
Diane Owens	DANTES
Wayne Patience	American Council on Education
Virginia Portlock	Chicago City Colleges
Wilburn Pratt	Kentucky Office of Vocational Education
Constance Queen	Mississippi Educational Television
Barry Semple	New Jersey Department of Education
Buell Snyder	Jefferson Co. (KY) Public Schools
Mary Williams	Indiana Division of Adult Education
Jerry Wilson	Kentucky Dept. of Adult Correctional Institutions